AF260953

This Book is
Protected by
Instant IP

NEVER CLIMB ALONE

How Entrepreneurs and Their Businesses Can Thrive with a Fractional CFO

NEVER CLIMB ALONE

How Entrepreneurs and Their Businesses Can Thrive with a Fractional CFO

A Business Fable
by Brad Martyn

ethos
collective

For business owners everywhere.
May you find your Sherpa.
And never climb alone.

Contents

The Sherpa People

The term *Sherpa* originally refers to a mountain-dwelling people native to Nepal. Over thousands of years in the rugged terrain of eastern Nepal, the Sherpa have developed genetic adaptations that enable their lungs to function more efficiently in the thin air of high altitudes.

Although they are renowned today for their mountaineering skills, Sherpas did not begin climbing the region's great peaks until the twentieth century. For generations, Sherpa families regarded the towering Himalayas as sacred—the dwelling places of the gods.

In 1953, Sir Edmund Hillary became the first known person to reach the summit of Mount Everest, accompanied by Tenzing Norgay, a Nepali Sherpa mountaineer.

Today, Sherpas take great pride in their mountaineering heritage. Their teams are legendary in the climbing world, guiding expeditions and helping climbers reach the summit of Everest.

They know the terrain, they've walked the path, they can shoulder part of the load—and they are there to help you *Climb the Mountain* and to make sure you *Never Climb Alone*.

Introduction

Over the past twenty-five-plus years, I have had the opportunity to sit down with hundreds of business owners. Maybe thousands. I've lost track.

Not professional managers hired to run someone else's company—but true entrepreneurs. The ones who get up every day, go to work with grit and determination, and shoulder the responsibility of building and running their own businesses.

These folks are the heart of the American economy, and I love them. I love that they create jobs. That they put their own capital at risk. That they sometimes go weeks, even months, without a paycheck. And most of all, I love the passion they bring to their work. Because they believe so much in what they are doing and why they are doing it.

Unfortunately, the statistics are sobering. Look up small business failure rates, and you will find no shortage of grim data—and long lists of reasons why businesses struggle.

But this book isn't about those stories. It's about helping businesses succeed. It's about encouraging business owners to focus on what they do best, build strong teams, and get the help they need—so they continue to love going to work every day and growing their businesses.

As you read, you will meet Rick, an entrepreneur, proud husband and dad, and the founder of RJ Enterprises. This is the story of his journey as a business owner, along with some of the challenges he faces. You will feel some of the loneliness he feels as an entrepreneur, too often walking alone.

You will also meet Kate, Rick's banker. Kate specializes in working with smaller, entrepreneurial businesses and is passionate about being more than their banker. She cares about her customers in a way that makes her a true, trusted advisor, and you will see what that means.

And you will meet Dean, an experienced Chief Financial Officer (CFO). After a very successful corporate career, Dean made the decision to become a fractional CFO. This allows him to bring his experience and expertise to small and medium-sized business owners, like Rick, who could never afford to hire someone with his background on a full-time basis, in a way that fits within their budget.

Kate and Dean are each passionate about helping business owners like Rick.

Their stories are told through the lens of my experience with FocusCFO, the fractional CFO company I founded in 2001, now an industry leader. Much of the story is about what I have personally experienced as an entrepreneur, business owner, business advisor, and CFO.

Before FocusCFO, I spent the first eighteen years of my business career mostly in corporate finance. Public and private companies, finance and operations, and lots of experience working directly with entrepreneurs.

At one point in my pre-FocusCFO life, I was heavily involved in the buy-side acquisition of seventeen companies over a twenty-four-month period. These companies' annual revenue ranged from $500,000 to $20 million. All were first-generation entrepreneurs who were running their businesses without a true CFO. Most of them were struggling with growth. All of them were wearing too many hats.

We completed each acquisition and, one by one, began integrating these entrepreneur-led businesses into the "culture" of our publicly traded company. The transition was difficult for each of them, but they soon saw the value an operationally focused CFO-led team could bring to their post-acquisition businesses. About a year after one deal closed, I visited one of the owners. He was struggling to adapt to the new "culture," which clashed with his entrepreneurial nature. He told me that now that he understood the difference between a CFO and a controller, he realized that if he'd had a CFO to work with before he sold, he wouldn't have done the deal.

My heart broke for him.

But that conversation sparked the birth of a business model in my mind—fractional CFOs.

While I certainly don't speak for the entire industry—there are many great fractional CFO companies and professionals beyond FocusCFO—I know I started FocusCFO for a reason. And the reason is for business owners like Rick, and for the advisors who help them succeed.

So, as you read about Rick, Kate, and Dean, you may recognize yourself or someone you know in one of them.

Because we always need to remember that no business owner should ever have to climb alone.

The Fractional Model: A Game-Changer for Growing Businesses

The fractional services model—where experienced industry professionals deliver strategic leadership to multiple companies on a flexible, shared basis—has been around for decades. But it gained real traction in the 2000s.

The term fractional CFO emerged during that time and has since expanded across the C-suite, including COOs, CMOs, CTOs, CHROs, and others.

Fractional services in each of these areas help smaller companies that can't afford or don't need a full-time C-suite executive. By working under a fractional arrangement, they gain the expertise of a C-suite executive for the time they need, at a cost they can afford.

However, because fractional had really started to catch on, the term fractional suddenly seems to be everywhere. And that's both good and bad.

Good, because of increased market awareness of the value a true fractional executive brings to the smaller business. But bad, because most people still don't fully understand what it really means, and that's often because the term isn't being used correctly.

Let's be clear: fractional isn't a buzzword, and it isn't a fad. Fractional is a specific business model—and it's here to stay. Fractional isn't consulting, interim, project-based, or temporary work. It's none of those. And it's certainly not like a traditional outsourced service.

Traditional outsourcing is deliverable- or report-based. You might outsource bookkeeping, marketing, payroll, data entry, tax preparation, HR, or IT. Your outsourced service provider handles a particular task or series of tasks, and in return, you receive a specific product or service deliverable or report.

Outsourced services are vital, and nearly every organization depends on them. But fractional is fundamentally different.

When you work with a fractional professional, you hire an individual (sometimes part of a fractional team) who works with you on a part-time, ongoing basis—essentially a fraction of a full-time executive. For example, a fractional CFO might spend one day a week working with your company, meeting with your leadership team, joining strategy meetings, and functioning as an integral part of your company.

Fractional work, in other words, is time-based. You get a certain amount of time each week or month. Deliverables follow naturally as part of the role. You see and work with the person just as you would with an in-house team member.

Unfortunately, because the term isn't regulated, "fractional" is now slapped on all types of services that have nothing to do with genuine fractional work. Many traditional outsourced service providers have begun rebranding their commodity services as "fractional" to capitalize on the trend. The result: confusion in the market about what fractional really means.

But those of us who have lived it know the difference. True fractional work involves an experienced executive—someone with years of industry expertise—who becomes part of a company's leadership team on a recurring, long-term basis.

Many fractional executives typically serve two to four companies each week. But just because they're not there every day doesn't mean they're not fully engaged.

At FocusCFO, we emphasize that fractional means our CFOs are embedded within the companies they serve. Being embedded means being involved in everything—from high-level strategy to day-to-day details—just like any other member of the leadership team. Others may define it differently, but this is how most experienced fractionals see it.

We also emphasize that true fractionals have worked IN industry, not FOR industry.

That's really important—and it's worth saying again:

Fractionals have worked IN industry, not FOR industry.

They're not traditional advisors offering opinions from afar or consultants doing project work. They're seasoned executives who've built real businesses and led real teams.

Fractionals bring the same insight, leadership, and accountability they once delivered in full-time roles—now scaled to meet the needs and budgets of small and mid-sized businesses. They learn each business inside and out.

It's like getting a multi–six-figure executive but only paying for 20–30 percent of their time.

As more business owners experience it, adoption will only continue to grow.

It's a complete game-changer.

No One Reaches the Summit Alone

In my years of sitting across the table from business owners, I've had the privilege of listening—really listening—to the hearts and minds of entrepreneurs.

They open up—sometimes slowly, sometimes all at once. They talk, and I listen. Some are looking for advice. Others want confirmation. But most just need a safe place to talk.

Because the truth is, entrepreneurship can be lonely. Who do you talk to when you're overwhelmed? Unsure? A little scared? Or when you just need someone to bounce ideas off of?

It's not always your spouse—especially when your home and personal assets are on the line. And it's not your employees—they expect you to have all the answers.

What business owners really need is someone with real-world experience who listens without judgment. Someone who asks good questions and doesn't rush to give advice or point out mistakes. A person with the wisdom to strike the right balance between insight and empathy—blending caution with encouragement.

Someone who listens 70 percent of the time and talks 30 percent.

Over the years, I've learned that what most business owners need isn't just advice or answers.

It's a guide.

A Sherpa.

Someone who has been there.

Someone with no agenda other than helping them reach their goals.

Someone who knows the trail can carry part of the load and help them climb the mountain.

That's what this book is about.

It's the story of a business owner—and a Sherpa.

Maybe you'll recognize yourself or someone you know in Rick, Kate, or Dean.

And maybe, just maybe, this could be your story, or their story, too.

The Story

1

Background

RICK'S STORY STARTS with Tom Miller.

Tom Miller started Miller & Co. over forty years ago. He had a reputation for delivering high-quality work, offering honest pricing, and providing outstanding customer service.

Tom is now sixty-eight years old and still comes to work every day. He always will.

When Tom's three sons, Andy, Steve, and John, each graduated from college, they began moving into roles within the company. And why wouldn't they? They were practically raised at Miller & Co.

From sweeping the floors when they were five or six years old, to cleaning equipment when they were ten, to riding in their dad's company pickup trucks—always white and always clean—for as long as they can remember.

Andy, the oldest, went to college and earned his MBA. Steve has a head for numbers and graduated with a degree in accounting. John, the youngest of the three, was the fun-loving, extroverted one, and he received his degree in business.

It was the perfect family combination for a second-generation family business.

Today, Andy runs the company and manages operations; Steve handles finance and accounting; and John, with an outgoing personality, takes care of sales. All second generation. All trained by their dad. All in their thirties and forties.

* * *

In high school, Rick Johnson worked on some summer construction jobs and discovered he had a talent for working with his hands. He enjoyed being outside, and he especially liked talking to people.

Rick joined Miller & Co. thirteen years ago, at twenty-two, just as Andy began running the company. Soon after Rick started working there, everyone found him to be both a hard worker and a team player.

As a young guy just starting out, Rick got to learn the business from the ground up. He spent several years with the production teams and loved it. He also had the chance to work on design and customer service. From there, he jumped into estimating and pricing. He loved it all.

As he grew in the business, Rick found his true passion was with customers. He went out on sales calls with each of Miller's top sales guys—always paying close attention and constantly taking notes.

Over time, Rick became a key player for Miller & Co. He was as good as they get—the best. The company rewarded him for his hard work with a good salary, great bonuses, and a company vehicle. With his earnings, Rick was able to provide for his wife, Annie, and their two children, Ryan and Emily, and put some money into their savings.

But after thirteen years with Miller & Co., thirty-five-year-old Rick was starting to get restless—he wanted more.

Rick always felt he was naturally entrepreneurial. That feeling grew over the years as he watched how the Miller family ran their business. What Rick loved was the passion they had for their work, a passion he didn't see in people who worked for big companies.

Being a business owner intrigued Rick. He at least felt he should be an owner in Miller & Co. However, things were a bit crowded around the kitchen table at the Miller home. There wasn't any room for someone with the last name of Johnson to be part of the Miller ownership team.

So, after much discussion with Annie, Rick came into work one Monday morning, walked into Tom's office, and told Tom he was leaving to start his own company.

Tom was devastated. Rick had become their top young talent and was critical to the business.

But Rick's mind was made up. He was leaving.

And a new entrepreneur was born.

2

Rick, the Business Owner

Five Years Later

RICK NEEDED A break. Actually, he needed more than that, but at that moment, he would be happy with just a break.

He was going to be late for dinner (again). And he was constantly missing things with his kids. Just last week, he missed Ryan's eighth-grade basketball game. The week before that, he missed Emily's piano recital. Oh, the joys of being a business owner.

For the first couple of years after leaving Miller & Co., things had gone well in his new business, RJ Enterprises. Really well.

Rick had numerous industry contacts and built a strong internal team. He loved the sales and business development side of the business and spent a lot of time there, at least in the beginning.

But as year one turned into year two and then year three, things started to get harder. Much harder.

Now, today, there were some real challenges. Rick was feeling pressure. More like heat. He always had a long list of things he needed to do to help the business, but something else would always come up. As a result, Rick was never able to spend time on what he wanted.

He found himself spending a lot of time dealing with issues he never had to at Miller & Co. He was constantly looking for updates on how the business was performing, from customer activity to production and delivery schedules. But the really hard one, the one he didn't expect when he started, was that he always seemed to be running short on cash.

Rick was now knee-deep, trying to get the bank what they needed to increase his credit line. His banker, Kate, had sent over the list of items needed to get the request reviewed and, hopefully, approved.

Sally—Rick's controller, bookkeeper, and office manager—sat with him at the round table in his office. It was mid-March, and as they reviewed the year-end financial reports, the numbers didn't make sense to Rick. He understood the numbers side of his business—pricing and production—or at least he thought he did. But accounting was a different way of looking at things, and the figures didn't align with how he thought the business had performed last year.

Sally tried her best to answer his questions, but a lot of it sounded like accounting speak to him. Accounting wasn't his thing, but he had been forced to try to figure it out. However, Rick had to admit to himself that he really didn't understand it, even though he confidently told people he did. He stared at the stack of reports on his desk.

His business was growing for sure. He knew that.

After a great first couple of years, sales continued to grow. Last year's sales were up almost 25 percent from the year before. However, the new work had stretched his production team and forced him to hire several more people. Some of the new orders seemed to overrun their budgeted cost—Rick wasn't sure by how much. He just knew he wasn't making as much money on them as he thought he would when he had submitted his pricing.

As he looked over the reports, he had questions.

Sally always got them done, but by the time Rick saw them, it was usually four or five weeks (or more) after the end of the month. By then, he didn't care all that much about the month the accounting reports were for. He was usually thinking about the next month and the month after that.

But today, as he looked over the numbers, he knew he had to send them to his banker, Kate. He had a lot of questions. Why did the income statement show positive net income, but he knew cash was tight? And how much in taxes was he going to have to pay by April 15? His CPA had not talked to him about his tax return, even though it was due in a few weeks. He knew from past years that his taxes were tied to his net income.

And then, with the new customers RJ Enterprises had just brought on board and production starting to ramp up, how was he going to pay his taxes in a few weeks and have enough cash in the bank to get these new customer accounts up and running?

And to make it even worse, he knew that over the summer, he needed to buy more inventory and hire a few more people.

He thought about the credit line. He already had loans totaling more than half a million dollars from the bank, which both he and Annie had personally guaranteed. This included putting their house and everything they owned up for collateral, which Annie was not happy about. Plus, he had already depleted most of their savings.

He didn't have to do that at Miller & Co.

And with all of that already done, why did the bank now want more information?

3

It's Starting to Rain

WITH A SIGH, Rick set aside the reports and glanced out the window while Sally walked back to her office. He thought about his business. Sales were strong, but he knew it was mostly luck. A few loyal customers just happened to call with several new, large orders. And then a couple of word-of-mouth referrals landed two new customers last year. So, while it looked good, Rick knew that wasn't going to happen every year.

Even with the new customers and orders, his prospect pipeline going into this year was not what he had hoped for. He hadn't had the time to spend with his customers or to try to bring in new sales orders. Instead, he spent most of his time trying to make sense of the numbers—and worrying about cash.

Rick was smart. Really smart. At Miller & Co., he consistently met the production schedule and budget. Back then, he knew the business like the back of his hand. No issues there.

But he was learning that this wasn't the same as managing a customer relationship or running a production schedule like he had done in his prior life. This was running a *company*.

Rick sat alone in the office. He sat back in his chair and stared out the window. It was now dark outside. His thoughts drifted to the two-day seminar in Chicago he was scheduled to leave

———

11

for tomorrow. He had signed up a few months ago when things were slow. Now that things were starting to get busy, he was having second thoughts. But he needed the break and the time away.

After working on a few things that were piled up on his desk, Rick turned to his computer and found an email from Kate, his banker. It took him three passes before he settled on his reply.

Hi Kate,

Thank you for your note. I am working with Sally to pull things together and should have everything ready for our 9 a.m. meeting on Monday morning at my office. I am heading out of town tomorrow for a couple of days to attend a seminar in Chicago that I signed up for a few months ago. I will be back Friday night. When we meet on Monday, I can show you what we have pulled together from last year.

The good news is that we have several new customers, and orders will start coming in next month. I am hoping you can let me know how much you can bump up my credit line. Plus, I need to purchase new equipment to accommodate the additional capacity for the new orders.

I will see you on Monday at 9 a.m. Enjoy the weekend.

Rick

He closed his computer, grabbed his bag, turned off the light in his office, and closed the door. He walked out the front door, locking it as he turned to the parking lot, which was empty except for his truck.

It was now almost 9 p.m.

The tension in Rick's shoulders and neck intensified. He had always felt pressure, but now it was pressure he felt he couldn't talk to Annie about—he wanted to be strong for his family. Despite his strength and determination, the pressure he felt was growing. It was different. He was beginning to think he might actually be in over his head and didn't know where to turn for help.

As Rick walked across the parking lot, it began to rain.

* * *

Rick quickly ducked into his truck to avoid getting soaked and headed home. Driving was therapeutic for him, especially when he had a lot on his mind. Music helped quiet the noise. He turned on the radio.

Bruce Springsteen.

"The Promised Land" was playing.

It was one of those songs about the hard road ahead. When you believe there is something in the distance, even when all of your hard work didn't seem to be paying off. About chasing a future that always seemed just out of reach.

Rick drove in silence, letting the song wash over him. His thoughts drifted, as they often did, to Annie—home again with the kids, spending her evenings alone while he chased the dream—a dream for him, and for his family.

The song was familiar—Rick had listened to it many times, for as long as he could remember. A song about doing your best, showing up every day, grinding forward even when the effort starts to bring you down. About moments when the pressure builds so much, it feels like it might bring you down.

He thought back to a conversation from just last week. Someone had asked how many hours a week he worked on the business.

"All of them," he'd said. And he meant it.

Rick eased the truck onto the shoulder of the road and shut off the engine, rain tapping against the windshield. He sat there, listening, feeling like the song was speaking directly to him.

Was he on the right track? Was he making a mistake? Had he pushed too far?

The long hours. The missed time away from his family. The constant weight he carried with him, even when he was home—and even then, he wasn't really home—he was thinking about work. Was it worth it? Was he building something real—or just running harder and harder toward something that kept moving away?

Everything they had was tied up in the business. Their savings. Their safety. Their future. And somehow, it still didn't feel like enough.

He sat there, thinking about where he was in his life.

And then the song shifted—not into easy answers, but into resolve. The reminder that he wasn't a kid chasing fantasies anymore. That believing in something—really believing— meant standing up to doubt and refusing to let it have the last word.

Rick wiped a small tear from his eye, put the truck into gear, turned right, and headed home.

The dream was harder than he ever imagined. Harder than anyone ever admits. He wanted to believe he was moving toward something meaningful—toward the version of success every entrepreneur pictures when they first take the leap.

But what he really needed now was someone to talk to. Someone who understood. Someone who could help him make sense of all of it.

He just wasn't sure who that was—or where to start looking.

4

Chicago

RICK DIDN'T THINK about what Chicago in March would be like when he signed up for the two-day seminar last fall, but he got lucky. When he landed at O'Hare on Wednesday afternoon, the weather was in the mid-forties. The snow was piled up on the side of the roads, but the sun was shining. Not bad.

As Rick checked into his downtown hotel and settled into his room, he pulled up the seminar schedule on his phone. He was looking forward to several interesting speakers, breakout sessions, and vendor presentations on Thursday and Friday mornings.

One session in particular caught his eye. It was during the last block on Friday afternoon when "How to Maximize the Value of Your Business" was being presented by an investment banker from Florida. He wasn't quite sure what an investment banker was, but he knew he had a banker he liked: Kate.

Rick hadn't started his business to sell it; he started it to run it. Selling wasn't his goal. Rick started RJ Enterprises because he wanted to make a difference, be his own boss, and focus on what he thought was important, both in the business and especially with his family. He had known some people over the years who had sold their businesses, so he was at least curious about what it was like to own a business with value.

He made a mental note about the session.

* * *

As the two-day seminar got underway, Rick found the Thursday workshops to be excellent. But by the middle of the afternoon, his phone was blowing up with texts.

First, there was a customer issue, followed by equipment problems. Then, Sally had some issues in the office. He texted back some responses and turned off his phone. If he wanted to get something out of this trip, he didn't need the distractions.

Thursday night, he called home. The kids were keeping Annie busy, but she was fine. Her attention kept returning to him, reminding him to make sure he got what he wanted out of the trip. She was the pillar of support. With all well at home, Rick focused on getting a few things done before going to bed.

Excitement for the next day's sessions was at the forefront of Rick's mind. On Friday morning, he planned to attend a demo of a new software system he wanted to explore for his business. And then, on Friday afternoon, came the keynote by the investment banker.

Before he went to bed, Rick opened his email and noticed a reply from Kate to his email from the previous day. The tension in his shoulders mounted again as his mouse hovered over the unread message.

While Rick loved working with Kate, he was a bit nervous about the meeting on Monday. With his new customers starting soon, he hoped Kate could expedite the credit line increase quickly and without much red tape, so he could get things moving with them.

Kate helped him secure the credit line and loans for his equipment when he started RJ Enterprises. During those initial conversations, she had told him that the credit line balance should increase during the summer and fall, but as things slowed down a bit in the winter, he should be able to pay it down to nearly zero. He could then borrow against the line in the spring, as things ramped back up, and pay it down again in the winter.

But for Rick, the line never seemed to go down. It just stayed maxed out. With a silent prayer, he opened Kate's email.

Rick,

I look forward to our meeting as well. I have two hours blocked off. Hopefully, that will give us enough time to talk about how things have been going. I have really enjoyed working with you for the last few years and getting to know you and your business.

I hope you enjoy the seminar. And please tell Annie I said hello.

Safe travels.

Kate

Rick finished reading the email. Two hours seemed like a long time for the meeting, but he knew Kate well enough that he trusted her. With those thoughts, he closed his laptop and went to sleep.

* * *

By noon on Friday, Rick was tired and ready to head home. While the sessions had been great and he had heard some new ideas that could help his business, he felt a bit overwhelmed. Plus, his phone kept buzzing with texts and missed calls.

His flight was scheduled to leave at 7 p.m., but there was an earlier one at 4 p.m. that he could make if he left early.

As he finished his lunch and started to pull his things together, he looked over the agenda, and the last session caught his eye again: "How to Maximize the Value of Your Business." His eyes darted back and forth between his watch and the agenda.

Curiosity and perhaps intuition won. Rick opened his laptop again and decided to stay.

5

Jack, the Presenter

AT 2 P.M., Rick headed back into the main room where the final session was scheduled. He was surprised that the room was packed. Every seat was taken. He looked around and found his usual spot near the back of the room.

The presenter, Jack Thomas, an investment banker from Florida, stood in front of the screen with his slides. Jack began his presentation by explaining that he wasn't a traditional banker who handled deposits and loans; his specialty was helping business owners sell their businesses. He was someone who helped you understand the value of your business and ran a process to identify potential buyers. If things went well, he then helped you sell your business.

It sounded to Rick a bit like a realtor helping you sell your house.

Then, Jack asked the audience a question. "So, who here is a business owner?"

The question made Rick perk up. He proudly raised his hand and, in doing so, looked around the room. Almost every hand in the room was raised. Not bad. All the vendors, accountants, and salespeople must have gone home by now.

The room quieted again as Jack stepped toward the group, the first slide from his presentation still in the background, "How to Maximize the Value of Your Business," and said, "That's great. Entrepreneurs are the lifeblood of our economy." He smiled, making eye contact with the audience, and then asked his next question. "How many of you have a CFO? A Chief Financial Officer?"

Rick was taken a bit aback. Steve was the CFO when he worked at Miller & Co., but that was a much larger company. At RJ Enterprises, he had Sally, who handled his accounting. She was kind of their CFO, so he raised his hand along with almost everyone else in the room.

Jack took another step forward. "I'm not talking about the office manager who does your bookkeeping, or a controller who does your accounting, or your outside CPA who does a financial statement. I am talking about a real, strategic CFO who knows your business inside and out, who understands your personal and business goals, and who matches your company's strategy with numbers."

Jack paused to let that sink in. Then he continued.

"Your CFO creates a financial roadmap and a financial plan to help you scale and grow your business."

Rick slowly pulled his hand down. Sally wasn't what Jack was talking about. While she handled the accounting and kept the books, she had no idea about strategy or the future. She did the historical numbers, but she never helped Rick understand what they meant, and she couldn't answer his questions.

Rick looked around the room. While he guessed there were about two hundred business owners in the room, only about ten still had their hands up.

Jack's last comment made everyone take notice when he said, "I promise you one thing. It is impossible to maximize the value of your business without a real, strategic CFO who knows your business inside and out, who understands your personal and business goals, and who matches your company's strategy with numbers."

The room was quiet. You could hear a pin drop. Jack sure got everyone's attention.

Rick made a note in his notebook.

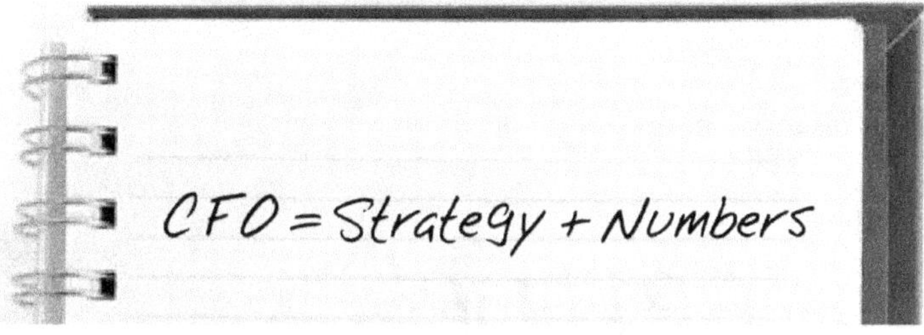

* * *

For the next ninety minutes, Jack took everyone through what a buyer looks for when purchasing a business and what a seller needs to do to ensure they get the right price when selling. He talked about strategic versus financial buyers, the importance of a strong management team, the need for scalable infrastructure, and the need for high-quality internal financial reporting and financial statements.

He walked through the importance of understanding gross margin and profitability by product and service. He used words like EBITDA (earnings before interest, taxes, depreciation, and amortization) and CapEx (capital expenditures)—both phrases

Rick had heard before but really didn't understand—and repeatedly talked about cash flow.

Rick divided his attention between the slides behind Jack and his notebook. He started taking more notes, jotting down key points and questions.

Jack's presentation discussed transaction multiples and the importance of minimizing business risk. He emphasized working capital, inventory turns, accounts receivable days, and forecasting cash flow.

Turns? Days? Working Capital? All these things were foreign to Rick.

He made more notes.

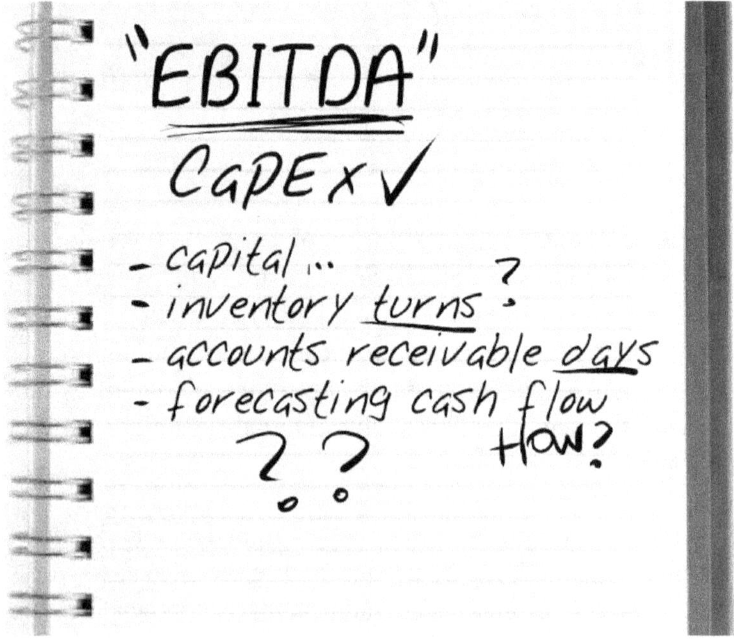

The one theme Rick kept hearing repeatedly was Jack talking about cash flow. He said that in smaller businesses, cash flow from operations was more important than EBITDA because it accounts for working capital.

What was cash flow from operations?

But what struck Rick most was that Jack never once said "net income." Not once.

Rick certainly knew what cash was, and he understood the basics of cash flow. But he never saw cash flow numbers on any of the accounting reports he got from Sally. Net income was always what Rick saw when he looked at his accounting reports.

He also thought back to all the discussions he had with his outside CPA. His CPA was great at taxes, and he always asked about sales and net income. He then worked hard to reduce RJ Enterprises' taxable income, so Rick would pay less in taxes.

And now Jack was talking about gross margin, cash flow, and how business valuations are based on higher earnings, not lower net income.

Rick shook his head. He was confused.

He had lots of notes.

And even more questions.

Author's Note

Little did he know, but Rick was one of the lucky business owners. He actually had an advisor—in his case, a banker—who truly cared about him and his business. And not because it helped her meet a sales goal or advance a personal agenda. In fact, it was the opposite. She never tried to sell him anything. She simply cared—about Rick and about how his business was doing.

It's rare. Too rare.

Most advisors do a great job answering questions when asked. They can explain their products and services and why they matter. That's expected—and appreciated.

But truly caring goes further. It shows up in three powerful ways.

First, great advisors make time for regular conversations—not just when deadlines are looming, or renewals are due, but simply to check in and see how things are going.

Second, they ask thoughtful, open-ended questions. Not just asking, "How's business?" but asking:

- "What's working and what's not?"
- "What are your biggest challenges right now?"
- "How are you doing personally?"

And then—and this is what separates them: they listen, they care, and then they act.

They have a complete help-first attitude, meaning they subscribe to what Bob Berg and John David Mann outlined in their groundbreaking book, *The Go-Giver*—that lasting success comes from focusing on providing exceptional value to others, and that authenticity and generosity ultimately create greater, long-lasting results. That, when you put others' interests first—by giving more than you take—success becomes a natural byproduct rather than the goal.

When they hear something outside their area of expertise, they connect the business owner with someone who can help. Not someone from their own company. Someone neutral. Someone right. Someone with special skills who can help.

Just like a good doctor who refers you to a specialist—not because they can't help, but because someone else can help better.

And that's exactly what Rick had.

The good doctor is in.

And she's walking through the front door.

6

Kate, the Trusted Advisor

AT 8:55 A.M. on Monday morning, Lori, the receptionist, buzzed Rick's office. Kate was here. Rick had been working with Kate for the entire five years he had been in business. He really liked her, and one thing he had learned was that Kate was always on time.

Lori walked Kate to the conference room and asked if she needed anything. Coffee? Water?

Kate was pleasant, looking right at Lori when she answered with a smile. "So kind of you to ask. I am fine, thank you. I will let you know if I need anything."

Lori returned the smile and left the room, while Kate took a seat at the conference room table, making sure she could see the door when Rick walked in.

At his desk, Rick gathered up a few reports he thought would be helpful. He had the income statement and balance sheet that Sally had printed for him from their accounting system. His tax return wouldn't be ready for several weeks, if he was lucky, and he hoped Kate wouldn't ask him about it.

As he stood up from his desk and turned towards the door, Rick thought back to the first time he had met Kate. His old boss, Tom Miller, had a great banker named Patrick Moore. Patrick had introduced Rick to Kate shortly after Rick told everyone he was leaving to start his own business.

Patrick told Rick that Kate was the best "relationship" banker he knew. At the time, Rick didn't exactly understand what he was talking about. But now, after running his business for all these years, Rick knew exactly what Patrick was talking about.

And as he walked towards his conference room, Rick started to count the number of times he could remember Kate meeting him at his office over the past five years. He couldn't remember them all, but he knew it was more than fifteen and probably closer to twenty.

Kate greeted Rick with a smile as she stood and shook his hand. He sat in his usual seat at the end of the conference room, exactly where Kate knew he would, while she sat in the seat at a ninety-degree angle from Rick. She always found that seating arrangement to be the best with her good customers. Not across from him and not directly beside him, but at an angle adjacent to him. She found it allowed for better conversation.

After asking some questions about the family and how the year was starting out, she asked, "So, how are you doing, Mr. Business Owner?"

Rick smiled. As soon as he heard her voice, he felt at ease. Because of the pressure he had been feeling about his credit line and the new orders he knew were coming up, his stress level was pretty high. But he was comfortable with Kate. She had a way of putting him at ease with the gentle way she asked questions.

Rick started to talk. It was March, and he had last seen her in November, just before the holidays.

He had a lot on his mind, including some of the things he had heard in Chicago last week.

* * *

Rick glanced up at the clock on the wall. It was nearing 11 a.m. Kate had mentioned in her email last week that she was blocking off two hours for the meeting, and the time sure had gone fast. But Rick was used to that. The meetings with Kate always seemed to go well.

Rick found that Kate was great at asking really good questions. Her questions were usually short, made Rick think, and were not so much about banking as about the business. When he first met her, he wondered if she had owned a business in the past (she said she had not). But for a non-business owner, she understood how Rick thought about things.

Rick mustered up the courage to ask about the credit line. He was disappointed when she didn't answer right away.

Kate took a moment and looked at Rick's balance sheet. She began asking questions that seemed similar to those Jack, the investment banker, had discussed at the seminar the previous week. Kate had asked about them before, but Rick didn't remember too much about what he had said in the past. That was back when his business was not quite as large, and before the company's revenue had grown so much over the past couple of years.

Kate asked Rick about some of his accounts receivable balances. Rick explained that most of those were from the bigger customers who were paying a little slow. "They will be fine," Rick said with a somewhat steady voice. Kate wrote something down.

Kate asked about some of Rick's equipment. She had helped Rick get financing on most of the equipment a few years ago. Rick handed her an equipment list. Kate skimmed down the list, asking questions as she read.

She asked about the utilization of his production equipment. Rick understood the concept really well, and they discussed it. Some of the equipment was used almost daily in production, while other pieces were more specialized and had been used only occasionally over the past few years for special orders. But Rick said he was glad he had them, in case they were needed for a future special order. Kate made a note.

Next, Kate looked through the financial reports. She asked Rick a few more questions. He didn't have as many answers as she had hoped. She asked Rick how often he saw the financials.

Rick admitted to Kate that he had looked at the accounting reports when he received them, but they were almost always late. He said that while Sally did her best, she was pulled in a lot of directions. Kate asked how well he understood the reports. She had asked that before, and Rick always said he understood them. But he sensed something was different about Kate's question this time.

Rick confessed, "I always thought I understood them, but now I'm not sure. And I sure am not an accountant." Then he added, "I tend to run the business based on what I see and hear. More of a gut instinct."

Kate put the reports down.

7

The Need For a CFO

KATE ASKED AGAIN how things were going with Rick, Annie, and the kids. Rick said things were fine but admitted that he wished he didn't have to work so much. Kate didn't seem surprised by Rick's comment.

Rick glanced back up at the clock. 11:45 a.m. The time had flown by.

As if reading the look on Rick's face, Kate said, "I am here for as long as we need to spend together." Next, Kate asked Rick where he was spending his time in the business.

Rick explained that he was always busy, but wasn't always sure what each new day would bring. He explained that when he started the company five years ago, he was doing what he loved. Back then, he was meeting with customers and prospects, spending time with his employees, and being a resource when needed.

Rick talked about how he always tried to be very visible. He knew his employees loved seeing him around the office and out in production. He was always full of encouragement, patting people on the back and telling them they were doing a great job. But over the past year, he hadn't been able to do that nearly as much as he wanted to.

Kate asked about meetings with customers.

Rick looked down and shook his head. "Not as much as I want. There are just so many things that I get pulled into."

Kate was quiet. The silence caused Rick to look away and think about his answer. He glanced back up at Kate.

Rick slowly admitted, "Okay. It seems that I rarely have time anymore to see a customer or prospect. There are certainly some new orders, but honestly, we were lucky to get them. Unless something changes, I don't think the growth is sustainable. And I'm worried we might even lose a big customer or two."

Kate was still quiet. When Rick didn't say anything else, she asked, "Rick, how much pressure are you feeling from the business?

Rick paused. It was a long pause.

He might as well say it. "A lot."

"What is your biggest challenge at this point?"

Rick was quiet. He trusted Kate completely. He realized this wasn't a meeting about the credit line. This was a meeting about Rick.

"Kate..." His voice started to quiver, so he took a moment to swallow. He hoped she didn't notice, but he was sure she did. "This is just so much harder than I thought it would be. I started this business because I was passionate about our industry and wanted to make a real difference. I knew I was good at it. And I know I can work hard." Rick nodded, showing his conviction. "But I have to admit, this isn't about the industry or just working hard. This is about business, and I'm not sure I am as good at that as I thought I was."

Kate leaned forward. "Rick, I've been your banker now for a long time. Ever since you started. I've watched you build this business from the ground up. You have done a great job so far." She offered a reassuring smile as she continued, "But I have been a banker for twenty-five years. I have seen many loans get approved simply because the bank was willing to approve them. But that didn't mean it was the best thing for the business owner—even when they asked for the loan."

The room was quiet for about fifteen seconds. Kate was thinking and carefully considering her next words. To Rick, it seemed like an hour.

"Rick, I can get you a credit increase. But not today. We need to get your business on a solid footing before we proceed. I don't want to see you and Annie get into trouble, or for something to happen that would affect your ability to continue running your business, or even keep it. You might even have to slow down your growth plan a bit."

After a moment to allow her words to sink in, Kate went on.

"I have someone you need to meet. His name is Dean Watson— he's a fractional CFO. I've seen Dean and his team do amazing things for several of the businesses we work with at the bank. They specialize in working with companies of your size, under a budget arrangement you can afford. I'd like you to meet with him."

Rick thought to himself, *A CFO? A fractional CFO?*

______

Rick reflected on the presentation in Chicago last week, when Jack asked, "How many of you have a CFO?" And then Jack's follow-up statement:

> *I'm not talking about the office manager who does your bookkeeping, or a controller who does your accounting, or your outside CPA who does a financial statement. I am talking about a real, strategic CFO who knows your business inside and out, understands your personal and business goals, and translates your company's strategy into numbers. They create a financial roadmap and a financial plan to help you scale your business.*

He remembered almost all of the hands going down, including his own.

Rick looked up. "But Kate, I'm sure I am too small to need a CFO, and I certainly could never afford one. Plus, I already have a CPA that I like. And why do I need a CFO? That has to be for much bigger companies.

He was worried about his cash, or his lack of cash at the moment. "But maybe if I really need one, I can just have Sally be my CFO."

8

Accounting vs. Finance

KATE SHOOK HER head. "First of all, a CPA and a CFO are completely different. CPAs handle your taxes and provide assistance with your accounting needs. They do lots of other great things, too, but their focus is primarily on reporting on what you did in the past. Plus, how often do you see your CPA?"

Rick said, "Well… I go over to his office every April to review my tax return. And he calls me sometimes." Rick looked away for a moment and then back at Kate. "But now that you mention it, that's probably it."

Kate continued, "CFOs are completely different from CPAs. I will walk you through that in a moment."

Rick nodded, Jack's words from the seminar still echoing through his mind.

"Secondly," Kate said as she tapped her pen against her pad of paper, "you can't just *give* Sally the title of CFO and have that be your answer. Having a CFO is not about a title. Titles are meaningless. It is about what the person actually does.

"Sally handles your accounting and the day-to-day administration, like billing and payables. She is great at what she does, and you are lucky to have her. But as it relates to accounting, she deals mostly with the past—things that have already happened. That is not at all what a CFO does. And giving Sally the title doesn't all of a sudden give her the ability to be a CFO."

Kate let that sink in, glancing down for a moment to give Rick time to digest what she had said.

After a few seconds, she looked back at Rick and continued, "Rick, I know a lot of companies that have a 'CFO' in title only. It's always someone who is really a controller, or even an office manager or bookkeeper. However, they lack the necessary skill set to be a CFO, so it never works. You can always tell because the business owner never has what they need to run their business the way they need to. Being a CFO is a combination of the right financial and operational experience and, more importantly, a specific mindset. The mindset is key. It is forward-looking and strategic. They understand your business, what your goals are, and they continually map out the financial roadmap for your business."

Rick nodded again. He knew she was right. He thought back again to Jack's words in Chicago when he said, *I am talking about a real, strategic CFO who knows your business inside out, who knows your personal and business goals, and who matches your company strategy with numbers.*

Same message from two different people: Jack and Kate.

Kate then explained, "There are three parts to the numbers side of your business: past, present, and future. Accounting deals with the past, as in what your CPA, controller, and bookkeeper do for you. The past. Yesterday's news."

Rick made a note. It was starting to make sense to him.

She continued, "Finance is strategic and deals with the present and the future. That is what a Chief Financial Officer does for you. CFOs are not about accounting. They are about finance. And finance is strategic and intentional."

Engrossed in the wisdom Kate was sharing, Rick scribbled some more notes without breaking eye contact.

She went on. "Business owners who don't understand the difference between accounting and finance pay a heavy price. Many get into so much trouble that they lose their business. The future needs to be planned for, versus just letting it happen."

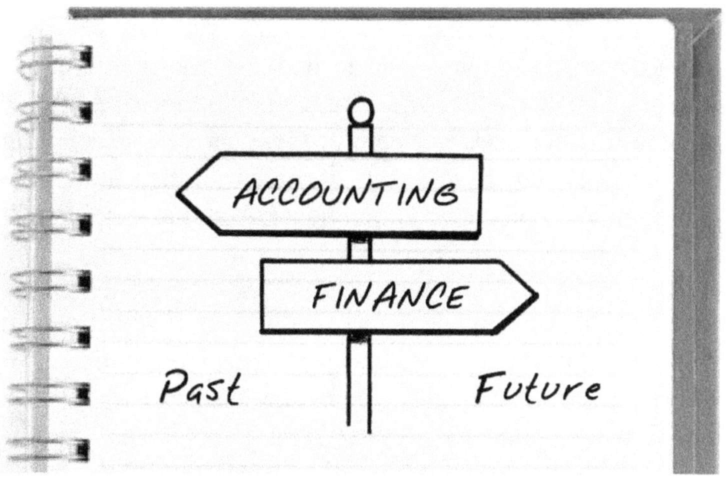

Planned future. Rick made another note in his notebook and underlined the words twice. He had never thought about his business in terms of planning for the future.

He always thought whatever happened, just happened.

She added, "Someone working as your CFO is meeting with you on a regular basis. At least twice a month, but often once a week. They are not there to do your tax return or just to review your accounting reports."

There was no judgment in Kate's words or tone.

"The best CFOs are embedded in your business and take care of all the financial matters in the company. Yes, they will work with Sally to make sure your accounting reports arrive with you each month on time, not late, and, most importantly, are accurate. But they are not here to focus on your accounting. Accounting should be less than 20 percent of their time. They are way more strategic and operational. And that should be 80 percent or more of their time."

Rick thought for a moment and finally said, "Well, trying to figure out all of that is what takes up so much of my time now. It keeps me from the sales side of the business, which is so important, and where we are struggling."

Kate nodded. "I agree, and on top of that, the real value of having your own CFO is that they take the time to understand you and your business. They become like a coach for you. Someone who knows your business way better than I do, who can become your confidante."

Despite the tightness in Rick's shoulders stemming from the practicality of hiring a CFO, the idea was resonating with him more and more.

"Having conversations with your CFO is not like talking to your employees or even with Annie or me. You can bring all your concerns to the table and discuss them with your CFO. They don't have any agenda other than to help you be successful."

Her smile softened as she added, "The really good ones have actually worked *in* business for twenty-plus years. Not working *for* business, like your CPA or even me. But *in* business. They have real-world experience, and they understand what you go through every day in a way that none of us on the outside ever could."

Rick was taking it all in.

Kate met Rick's gaze with determination. "I really feel now is the right time for you, Rick. Your business is growing and in a great place, but there is a lot to do to take it to the next level—both for the business and for you personally. Are you okay if I make an introduction this afternoon?"

Rick was shifting from apprehension to excitement. "Of course. If you think I need to, I will meet with him."

"That's great, Rick," said Kate. "I know you will enjoy talking to Dean."

She asked Rick if there was anything else he wanted to talk about. Rick said no, and he thanked Kate for spending so much time with him. As always, he loved it when she stopped by. Now he had a lot to think about—more than usual.

They each stood up, shook hands, and Kate headed out. As always, she said goodbye and waved to Lori as she walked out the front door.

* * *

———

Within an hour, Rick saw an email from Kate.

Rick,

Thank you for meeting with me today. I promised I would introduce you to Dean Watson. Dean is with the fractional CFO group I mentioned.

Hi Dean,

Rick Johnson is a client of mine with whom I just met. He is the founder of RJ Enterprises. Please reach out to him to arrange a meeting time. He is excited to talk with you.

Would each of you keep me posted on when you are meeting and how things are progressing? I know you will enjoy meeting each other.

Thank you,

Kate

Rick looked up and glanced at the picture of Annie and their two children on his desk. He picked it up and stared at it for a few seconds.

As he sat down at his desk, he flipped back in his notebook to his notes from Jack's presentation last week.

It is impossible to maximize the value of your business without a real, strategic CFO who knows your business inside and out, who understands your personal and business goals, and who matches your company's strategy with numbers.

Perhaps Dean was someone he could discuss Jack's comment from last week and some of the things weighing on him about the business with. He looked up and glanced at his computer. He found Kate's email and hit "Reply all".

Kate – Thanks for stopping by. You always have great ideas, and I really value your insights!.

Dean – I look forward to meeting you. I can be flexible pretty much any day later this week or early next week. Just let me know what works best for you.

Rick

Rick had only a moment of relief before Lori walked in with messages from seven people who needed to talk to Rick right away.

9

Dean, the Fractional CFO

DEAN HAD BEEN quick to reply to Rick's email. He thanked both Rick and Kate, and asked Rick what day worked best for him.

Rick saw the email on his phone. He replied that Friday at 9 a.m. would be perfect.

* * *

On Friday morning, Dean walked up to Lori's desk in the reception area a few minutes before nine. As Lori called for Rick, she noticed that Dean was looking closely at some of the framed photos in their lobby. They were all photos of products RJ Enterprises made and customers they had worked with over the past few years.

Lori walked Dean back to the conference room, the same one where Kate had met with Rick earlier that week. The room had chairs for a dozen people to sit around the table, and Dean found the seat he wanted: the one facing the door, right next to where he thought Rick would sit at the end of the table. It was the same seat Kate had sat in.

He put his small notebook on the table and walked over to look at some more pictures on the wall.

Rick walked in, said hello to Dean, and shook his hand. After they were both settled, Dean started by asking about Kate and how long Rick had known her. He asked what he thought of her. Dean knew the answer. Kate was special, and Rick was lucky to have her as his banker.

The conversation remained light as Rick and Dean discussed their families, where they were from, and what they enjoyed doing in their free time. Dean was a golfer, and so was Rick, although Rick admitted he wasn't very good. But he said he liked to get out and play a few times a month when he wasn't too busy. But then Rick admitted that for the last few years, he hadn't had time to play at all.

Dean then asked a series of easy questions that Rick was more than happy to answer. "So, how long have you had your business?" "What did you do before this?" "How many people do you have working for you?"

Finally, after the two had established rapport, Dean got down to business. "So, what's it been like starting your own business after working with an established company for so long?"

Rick leaned forward in his seat and considered his response. He usually just told people how great it was, but there was something about Dean that made Rick think harder about how he wanted to respond. Maybe it was because Kate had asked Rick to meet with Dean that Rick felt more comfortable with him than with some other people who had sat at his conference room table over the years.

He decided to open up. "It was fun in the beginning. I was doing everything I wanted to do. As we started to grow, it was harder for me to keep track of things. I used to know intuitively how much profit we made on each of our customers, products, and services. Then, as we got bigger, I still thought I knew the profitability of what we did."

Dean nodded as he listened to Rick.

"But now, when I get reports from Sally, they don't make sense to me. The top-line sales number is usually fine, but the bottom line rarely makes sense to me. And the expense categories on the accounting reports never align with how I think about the business."

Silence lingered in the room for several moments. Dean was patiently waiting for Rick to say everything that was on his mind.

"Today, I *think* I am okay, but honestly, I'm not sure." Rick's shoulders lifted in a defeated shrug. "I have a couple of new customers getting ready to start, and I really needed the bank to increase my line of credit. But when I met with Kate, she didn't just tell me I could get the increase. She said she thought I needed help, and that's why we are sitting here."

10

Rearview Mirror vs. GPS

DEAN LISTENED CAREFULLY. He quietly reflected on some of the things he had seen during his thirty-year career in finance and operations. While he started his career in accounting, he quickly moved into finance and operations. He was familiar with Rick's industry, but certainly not an expert at it. He was well-versed in nearly every aspect of business, finance, accounting, and operations.

In his role as CFO, Dean often heard people discuss revenue and net income. That was what Rick was talking about. But Dean knew that gross margin and operating cash flow were critical in every business. Gross margin was usually more important than sales. And, despite what every accounting system told you, net income was, for the most part, irrelevant.

As one of Dean's mentors had taught him, *"You don't pay the bills with net income."* It was operating cash flow that was king.

Dean knew from their brief conversation that Rick was smart and understood his business. He also quickly realized the accounting information Rick was getting from Sally wasn't intuitive to Rick or how he thought about the business—he was only getting accounting information. It was purely historical. Nothing was forward-looking.

It was like driving a car, constantly looking in the rearview mirror.

There was no roadmap, no GPS, nothing financial that gave Rick a forward-looking view. That is what finance does. It shows the path forward—like a GPS—focusing on the most important aspect of Rick's business, or for any business: cash flow.

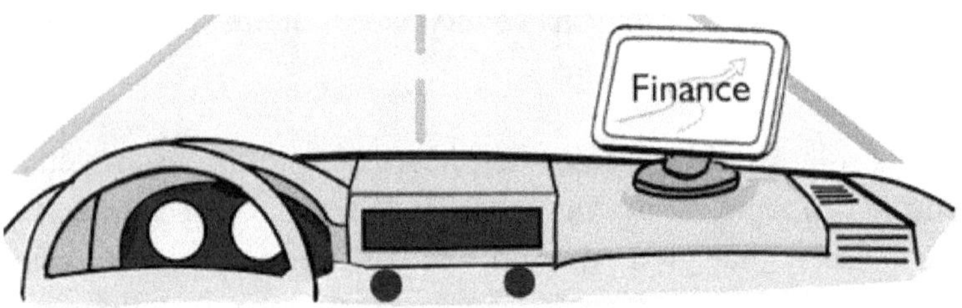

Dean asked how much control Rick felt he had over the finance side of the business.

Rick replied, "Well, I am not an accountant."

Dean smiled. "Well, I didn't say accounting. I said finance."

Rick sat up. "Can you tell me the difference?"

Dean said, "A lot of business owners think they are the same. But they are not. Finance is way more than accounting. *It is business*. It has to do with how you price your products and services, as well as understanding the profit margins on everything you do.

"It includes metrics and key performance indicators that tell you if you are having a good day, or week, or month, well before you ever see any accounting reports. It is having a solid understanding of your cash flow—today and into the future."

Rick jumped in, "So, that's why you said, '*It is business*, not accounting'?"

Dean nodded. "Right. But don't get me wrong. There is absolutely a role for accounting. It is critical and has to be accurate. Accounting is foundational for every company. But let me ask you, Rick, how much time do you spend a day thinking about how your business did last month, or last year, versus how it is going to do this month or this year?"

"100 percent this month and this year," Rick replied without hesitation.

"So, what financial information do you have that helps you with that?"

There was a brief silence, followed by "I never really thought about that before."

11

The Three Building Blocks

DEAN SAT BACK and said, "Let's shift gears a bit, Rick. Let me sketch something out for you."

Dean walked to the whiteboard in the conference room and grabbed a marker. He drew three rectangular boxes side by side on the board. In the left one, he wrote Revenue. In the middle one, he wrote Production. In the one on the right, he wrote Finance/Admin.

Rick copied down what Dean wrote on the board.

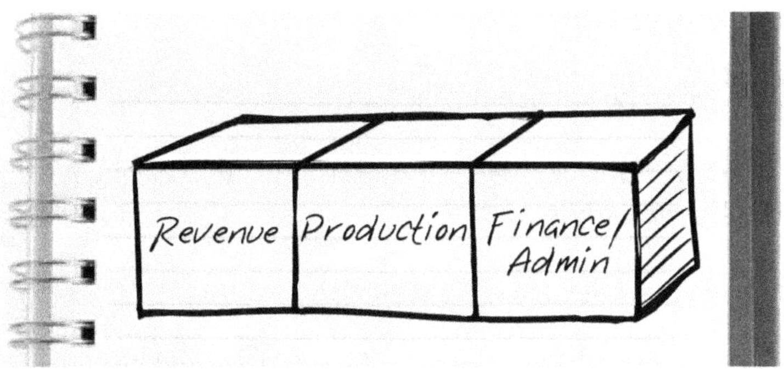

He then asked Rick to think about where he spent his time as a business owner in each of these three key building blocks of every business: revenue, production, and finance/admin.

Dean explained that revenue encompassed everything related to acquiring customers, including sales and marketing. Production encompassed all activities that support what was sold, including operations and customer service. Finance/Admin was primarily about the money side and everything else that didn't fall under the other two.

This one was hard for Rick to answer. It was hard because intuitively, Rick knew the answer, but he didn't want to admit it.

Seeing the hesitation, Dean tried a different approach. "Let me ask it this way. Where did you spend your time in the first couple of years?"

That was easier. Rick was quick to say that revenue was at least 60 percent. "It had to be. Without sales, there was no business."

"Great, that makes perfect sense," said Dean. "Where else?"

"Production was probably 30 percent, and finance/admin was maybe 10 percent."

Dean asked how much fun that was.

"A ton," said Rick, his eyes flickering with excitement as he recalled the early years.

"So, what's it like today?" asked Dean.

Rick looked back at his calendar for last week and then glanced at this week's calendar. It was Friday, and he couldn't think of a single important work-related thing he had gotten done all week, other than his meeting with Kate on Monday.

Rick said, "It has to be the exact opposite. Revenue is 10 percent in a good week." Although Rick couldn't remember the last sales-related thing he had done.

"Production is still around 30 percent," Rick said. "But whereas in the early days, I was working on production design and new products, today it is mostly putting out fires. And then the rest of my time seems to be chewed up with all of the administration and numbers stuff that I don't like or don't understand."

And before Dean could say anything, Rick said, looking away, "And before you ask, I am not having any fun anymore."

12

What Do You Do Best?

DEAN SMILED. HE then asked Rick what the one thing was that Rick did better than anyone else. Something that was critical to the business and that Rick was really passionate about.

Rick thought for a second. No one had ever asked him that before. "It has to be meeting with potential or existing customers to generate more revenue. I am good at it, and I enjoy doing it. Plus, no one else on my team can do it like I can."

Dean weighed in and said, "As the owner of the business, you have credibility with potential customers and current customers, correct?

Rick was trying to be humble. "It would seem so," said Rick.

Dean tilted his head a bit and gave Rick a moment to say more.

"Okay, yes, for sure," said Rick.

Dean looked directly at Rick. "We are going to talk a lot about this in the future. That is called your Unique Ability."

He then asked, "So I am curious, has anyone ever talked to you about this before?"

Rick shrugged his shoulders. "No. No one. I've not heard any of this before."

Dean went on, "Let me take you through what I've learned about it. Just jump in as this starts to make sense to you."

"Dan Sullivan is the founder of Strategic Coach and an extremely successful business coach and author. He coined the phrase 'Unique Ability' years ago, and his research in this area was groundbreaking. He taught that your Unique Ability is something you love to do that produces great results."

Dean continued, "I have found that in the case of many entrepreneurial businesses, it is often something that no one else in your company can do as well as you can. So, when I think about an entrepreneur's Unique Ability, I often first think of sales and marketing. Why? Who else knows your product or service better than you, and who is more passionate about what you do than you?"

"That would be the case with me," replied Rick.

Dean then said, "Knowing that sales and marketing are the lifeblood to any business, I find that way too many business owners want to hire someone else to do it. In my experience, that is one reason so many businesses struggle or even fail. As the business owner, you can't step away from the single most important thing in your business, especially if it falls into your Unique Ability."

Rick thought about it. "It's funny to hear you talk about that. I know some business owners who think they can hire someone to handle everything related to revenue generation, meaning all of sales and marketing, and then not be involved in it at all."

"And how did that go for them?" asked Dean.

"Almost always not that great," said Rick.

"Now don't get me wrong," said Dean. "Salespeople play an important role in every growing company. You can't grow without them. But when business owners step away from sales and marketing altogether, it usually doesn't go very well. Then, over time, they get frustrated at the lack of sales success and start to blame others."

"I can see that," replied Rick, nodding.

"Just to make sure it's clear, having a Unique Ability around sales and marketing doesn't mean you are a cold caller," Dean explained. "It means you are great with customers, you are passionate about what you do, and you have a hunter mentality. You want to get up every day thinking about revenue and how to grow your business.

"You then need to determine how to leverage those skills, be actively involved, and contribute to driving revenue for your company. I've seen business owners do it in different ways. That's fine. There are many different ways to do it. Just be actively involved and don't try to hire someone else to do it all. Does that make sense?"

Rick nodded, "I know exactly what you mean."

13

Running Your Company

THE QUESTIONS CONTINUED to evolve as Dean asked Rick about how he ran the company, his employees, the business's structure, and the types of meetings they held.

Talking about his employees was easy for Rick. He certainly knew everyone, what they were good at, and what they did for the company.

"Tell me how your company is structured," inquired Dean.

"Well, we don't have an organizational chart," replied Rick.

Dean smiled.

Rick continued, "In the beginning, everyone reported to me, which was great. It was actually pretty easy for me. I had my hands in everything, and I trained everyone to do things the way I wanted them done.

"Then, as the business grew, I found I had to spend more time with certain people because they weren't able to take on more responsibility. They were good at what they did – to a point. That's when it started to get harder."

Dean nodded and let Rick continue.

Rick went on. "It was hard because I had to spend time in areas that I really didn't want to, and it pulled me away from what I wanted to do. Over time, I realized I needed to bring in more experienced people, and I've done some of that, but not as much as I need to. I have great contacts in the industry and know lots of people, so finding good people isn't the issue. It's frustrating at times that some of my original team members can't grow with the company. I have been really loyal to them because they have been with me since the beginning. And I know how hard they have worked for me over the years."

Dean made some notes, and Rick opened up more. He noticed that as Rick went on, he seemed to describe things more in terms of employees and what they did than in terms of how the business operated or should operate. He made a note of that.

Rick finally said what Dean was waiting for. "They are almost all still here, but not playing as key roles as I had hoped they would be playing at this point."

"It's interesting that you mention roles," Dean said. "We will come back to this later, but I want us to start thinking about the business more in terms of the roles or the functions needed, versus the people that are here. One way to do that is to imagine you were starting the business today, with your current customer base, selling the products and services you offer today, and ask yourself how you would set things up, knowing what you know today. But, again, we will come back to that. I just want to plant the seed for you to start to think about it."

Rick made a note in his notebook.

Dean then asked about annual planning sessions, quarterly sessions, and even weekly meetings. Rick said he wasn't a fan of meetings at all, except for customer review meetings, where they do a deep dive into the status of each order against the production schedule. Rick could talk about that all day long.

Dean said, "That is certainly important, and it's great you do those, but I am talking about things at a higher level—for the company as a whole. Focusing on things that move the business forward versus getting current orders out the door."

Rick seemed a bit confused by that. In his mind, getting each order out on time and within budget was the key to the business.

Dean went back to the board, wrote "Operating Rhythm" above the three boxes he had drawn before, and drew a circle around everything. Rick did the same.

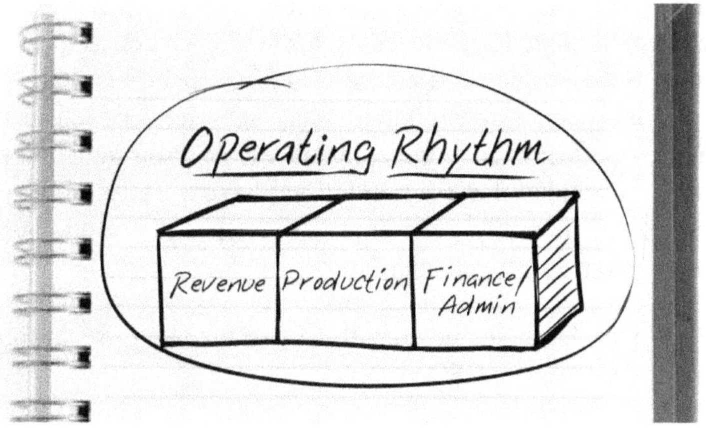

He then said, "The meeting you are talking about, where you review current orders, is an operational meeting, not a leadership meeting.

"What I am referring to is a leadership meeting involving the key people who run the revenue, production, and finance/ admin functions, as well as you, Rick, as the company's leader.

The goal here is to identify six to eight key initiatives each quarter that will move the business forward and align everyone's efforts to accomplish the company's goals.

"That meeting is part of the company's overall Operating Rhythm."

Rick again shook his head and said this was all new to him.

Dean made a note and decided to step back a bit.

* * *

Dean asked a few more general questions and listened closely as Rick talked. They were questions that made sense to Rick, but no one had ever asked him before. Some of the questions were personal to Rick: his goals, his family, where he spent his time in the business, where he wanted to spend his time, and what he was passionate about. Dean then transitioned to the leadership team. They talked about each person individually. Dean concluded that Rick didn't yet have a leadership team. He had some really good employees, but they weren't functioning as a leadership team.

After that, Dean shared something that made him seem more like a coach than a CFO.

Dean said, "I want to summarize some of what we have talked about today and talk about some next steps. First of all, Rick, you have done an amazing job getting your company started. You have a great brand and some really good employees. But let me ask you a question: When was the last time you stepped back and looked at your business from the outside?"

Rick paused. "From the outside? Honestly, it's been a while. Maybe never."

"Exactly. When you're in the details every day, it's tough to see where you're actually headed. I also think you might agree that you are starting to hit some ceilings, where things are getting hard."

Dean looked at Rick, and Rick nodded. "And my head sure is starting to hurt from hitting the ceiling so many times."

They both laughed.

Dean continued, "Rick, I see it all the time—and it's normal—and it happens to the best of business owners. What starts out as a vision and passion can, over time, turn into something that the business owner doesn't even recognize. The running of the business becomes overwhelming and, to put it bluntly, just not fun anymore."

Rick said, "Well, I'm there."

14

Dean's Three Keys to Success and Getting Started

DEAN JUMPED RIGHT back in. "Rick, in my experience, both in running a business and working as the right-hand person to business owners, I have found there are three keys to success for business owners. We have touched on each one of these, but let me simplify some things for us.

"The first is for you, as the entrepreneur and business owner, to spend at least 60 percent of your time every week on your Unique Ability. Later, you will shoot for 100 percent. But for now, because you have your hands in so many things, I want you to start with a goal of 60 percent."

Rick was taking notes.

"The second is that you need to have Full Financial Control over every aspect of your business—past, present, and future. That gets into the financial aspects we talked about.

"And then third, you need to get the business operating under a regular Operating Rhythm—a regular system or process of running your business, versus reacting to it all the time. This is where your leadership team really comes into play."

Three keys, thought Rick. He sketched each one as Dean spoke, making notes to the side. When Dean finished, Rick underlined the heading.

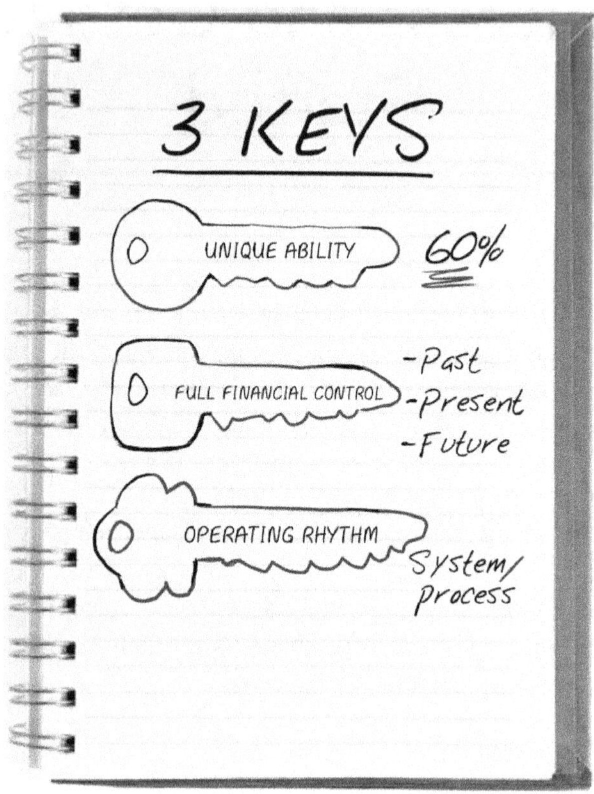

Dean explained that if they decided to work together, these three things would serve as the basis for everything they did.

Rick finished writing, looked again at his notes, and said, "It all makes sense to me. So, let me ask, what's the next step?"

Dean said, "Well, that depends on two things. What you want at this stage of your business, and then if it makes sense for us to work together."

To which Rick replied, "I just want to enjoy working in my business again. And yes, I would like to have your help in getting me to where I want to go."

Dean smiled. "That's what I wanted to hear you say. Let me tell you how this works."

* * *

Dean told Rick that, as a fractional CFO, he worked with only a handful of businesses. The time with each business varied based on their needs, but it was always on a recurring schedule, with him there every week.

For Rick, based on his size and needs, Dean said one day a week was the right amount of time. That would allow the two of them to spend time together each week, for Dean to work closely with Sally and others on the leadership team, and for Dean to tackle issues and projects he and Rick felt were important.

Dean said one of his primary goals was to give Rick two things: time and information.

It was clear that Rick was spending time in areas that were not productive—for Rick or for the business. It was also apparent that Rick didn't have the right information to effectively run his business.

Dean's goal was to give him back both—time, so he could focus on the right areas. And information—good financial and operational information—that would allow Rick to run the company more professionally and more effectively.

Rick made another note.

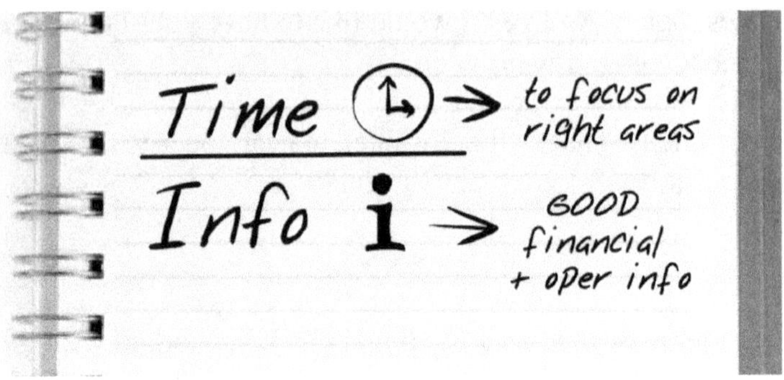

To do this, Dean would become embedded in the business and a key member of Rick's leadership team. He would work mostly on-site at Rick's office on a designated day each week, but would be accessible throughout the week if time-sensitive issues arose. But they would make sure to do the bulk of their work during Dean's scheduled on-site day each week.

Rick nodded that he understood.

Dean discussed working within ninety-day planning cycles. Collectively, Dean and Rick would develop an issues list of things they felt needed to be looked at or addressed. They would then tackle two or three of the most important ones every ninety days. Rick liked that. Two to three issues at a time seemed manageable and something he could handle. Rick was excited about the changes but also knew he had a business to run. He really liked that Dean understood the need to pace themselves and take things one step at a time.

Dean also explained that he wasn't a magician. Things would take time. Certainly, there would be some "quick wins" they would knock out. But real change takes time. And even though Rick could cancel their arrangement at any time, he needed to commit to working hard at this for at least two years if he wanted to see real change. Dean mentioned that most of his other clients had worked with him for at least five years, and they were still going strong.

Rick nodded again.

As Dean talked, one thing that stood out to Rick was that they would meet one-on-one each week. Here, they would update each other on what was happening in the business, discuss the progress of open items, and address any new issues that had arisen since the last meeting.

Rick really liked talking to Dean and was excited that he might have finally found the person he could open up to about business issues.

Another thing Rick liked was that Dean wanted to come to Rick's office for half a day and have one-on-one meetings with the key members of Rick's team—those he would regularly work with—*before* Dean actually started working with Rick. Dean explained that he didn't want anyone to be surprised when he showed up for the first day. Similar to what he asked of Rick, Dean also wanted their buy-in to work with him. Plus, the time would give Dean a chance to ask them questions and get a sense of their issues and how they did their jobs.

Rick liked everything he was hearing.

Then Dean said, "Rick, one more thing. And this is important."

"Sure, anything," said Rick. He leaned forward a bit.

"First of all, I have to tell you the key to all of this will be how coachable you are."

He looked at Rick to make sure that it had sunk in. After a few seconds, Rick acknowledged that it had.

"And second, I don't know your industry like you do. I never will. But I will learn from you and get pretty good at it. But this isn't about your industry. It is about business."

Dean went on, " I am going to bring new things to the table that you have never heard of before. Not all of them will be things we decide to implement. But many of the ones we decide to put in place are going to require you to change. Some of this will take you out of your comfort zone. You just need to be ready for that."

Rick appreciated the honesty. He was ready.

* * *

They had the meeting with the team the next week, and Dean started the following week.

Rick officially had his own CFO.

15

A CFO with Experience Working IN Industry Not FOR Industry

DEAN WAS EXCITED about working with Rick. He felt they hit it off and would work well together. He could tell that Rick wanted to learn, and he believed Rick when he said that he was coachable. That was important.

As a fractional CFO, Dean had achieved considerable success working with entrepreneurs. One reason he had become a fractional CFO was that he had grown tired of the corporate grind. Working for larger companies for the first twenty-five years of his career had been great. He had incredible financial and business mentors, who were key to his development as a CFO.

During his corporate days, he traveled extensively across much of the US and to some international destinations. He had been exposed to professional managers and entrepreneurs and learned from each of them. He had strong skills in financial analysis and worked closely with attorneys, bankers, and CPAs. He had been involved in acquiring several companies throughout his career, which provided him with tremendous insights.

Dean was known as a CFO who could walk the shop floor one day and give a presentation in the boardroom the next. He was heavily involved in strategic planning, but his real passion was operations.

During his time as a corporate CFO and finance executive, Dean had always spent time on the operations side. He knew the only way to be an effective CFO was to fully understand the business inside and out. He was naturally drawn to the people on the production floor and enjoyed walking through manufacturing facilities and project sites. He knew these were the people who really did the work.

The sales guys loved him, too, because he understood the importance of sales and marketing. He knew that without sales, there would be no operations and no finance.

He loved the passion entrepreneurs had for their businesses and what they did. That was one reason he was attracted to the fractional CFO model. He wanted to help business owners realize their dreams and be in control. It just so happened that his expertise in finance was the Achilles' heel for many business owners.

Dean had read Michael Gerber's book, *The E-Myth Revisited: Why Most Small Businesses Don't Work and What to Do About It*. It helped Dean understand that technicians—people skilled at a craft—don't naturally make successful entrepreneurs. Their technical expertise too often gets in the way of running a successful business.

The *E-Myth* outlined for Dean why so many small businesses fail. It emphasizes building a business that thrives by working "on" the business rather than "in" the business. That resonated with him.

Dean found that concept difficult for many entrepreneurs to grasp. It was counterintuitive.

Many entrepreneurs initially succeed by working hard and making sure everything gets done. Long hours were the answer, at least in the beginning. However, as their businesses begin to grow, hard work is no longer enough, and no one person can do everything. The entrepreneur needs to start focusing on what they do best, and often, those are things that only they can do.

Too many people fail miserably by not working "on" their business, often because they simply couldn't get out of their own way and were always working "in" their business.

But Dean loved the skilled operators—the technicians that Michael Gerber talked about. He wanted to help them succeed and realize their dreams.

He also felt working with Rick would complement the other businesses he worked with as a fractional CFO. They were all, for the most part, in different industries. That didn't bother Dean at all. Business was business, and the principles were the same.

Additionally, many of the ideas and concepts he learned at one company brought fresh perspectives to the others. Whether it was implementing incentive compensation plans, working with tax CPAs, or simply understanding the DNA of a business.

He wouldn't have it any other way.

* * *

Rick and Dean jumped in and got started. Dean learned the business and brought new insights to Rick and the team. All the things he told Rick he would do.

As Rick learned, he grew tremendously. He let go of things he didn't think he would. But the trust was there with Dean.

And as Dean rolled up his sleeves, things started to come together.

There were some quick wins, just as Dean had mentioned.

But the real work would require change.

It didn't happen overnight, just as Dean said it would. But it happened.

16

Getting to Work

AS DEAN GOT started, he worked hard for the first several weeks to understand Rick's business.

To do that, he started at the beginning—with sales.

He wanted to understand how customer orders came in. He needed to determine whether the sales process was proactive (meaning the sales team worked to get new customers and new orders) or reactive (more like a customer service business, where the sales team simply answered the phone as calls came in).

He found it was both, which was good.

Then came production. Dean wanted to understand the purchasing process and how inventory was ordered. When he spoke with the warehouse manager, he found that much of the inventory was ordered simply because the warehouse racks were empty, not because they believed they could sell it. Dean noted that—it explained, in part, why the inventory balance on the balance sheet was so high.

He asked for an "aged inventory report." This would show inventory by line item, how many of each item were in RJ Enterprises' warehouse, and how long each item had been in stock. This was similar to an accounts receivable aging report, with columns for under 30 days, 31–60 days, 61–90 days, 91–180 days, 181–365 days, and over 365 days. But Rick's system wouldn't produce it, and that was problematic.

Dean needed to know how much inventory had been in the warehouse for more than six months. That was almost always the root cause of tight cash flow in a business with inventory.

He understood that, for most inventory items, sound business practice was to buy what you knew you could sell and sell it quickly. This was measured in "turns," or how many times per year you turned over or sold each item. More turns were always better.

Dean liked to joke that how inventory is managed is often the difference between running a business and running a museum—a museum is full of stuff that doesn't sell.

As Dean walked through the warehouse, he knew the answer. He looked for dust on the inventory on the racks. That meant the items had been there for a while. That wasn't good.

He also found that the farther back in the warehouse he walked, the dustier the items he found. Slow-moving inventory often hid in the back. He made lots of notes.

Dean then went to the production area and talked to the people who actually did the work. Dean was always comfortable talking to them—he spoke their language. They could tell he was genuinely interested in what they did. Dean asked questions, and he listened—he really listened—to their answers. And he took more notes. He always thanked them for talking with him.

Over time, as he spent more time in production and talked to them more, he learned about their families and hobbies. He formed a bond with them.

Dean certainly wasn't just a numbers guy.

He followed the product through the entire process—from how each order was received, to how inventory was ordered, to how it flowed through production and work-in-process, to finished goods, and ultimately to shipping. Dean was impressed. Rick had done a great job with all of this, but Dean's experience helped identify several areas to work on.

From Dean's CFO standpoint, he was looking at the cash cycle. He wanted to understand when RJ Enterprises spent cash, when it received cash, and how long that cycle lasted on a typical order. Dean's job was to help shorten that cycle.

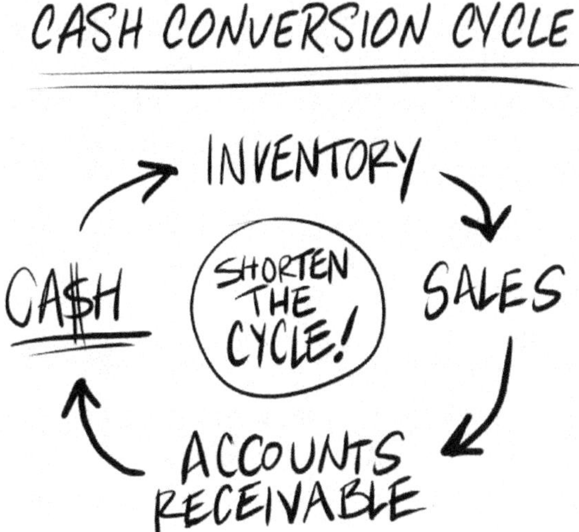

He especially wanted to minimize the amount of slow-moving inventory in the warehouse. To Dean, slow-moving inventory represented stacks of dollar bills just sitting on a warehouse shelf.

It always struck Dean as interesting that businesses would borrow money on their line of credit, buy excess inventory that sat on their shelves—not selling, not moving, not "turning"—and then ask the bank for a bigger line of credit. Why? Too often, the answer was to buy even more slow-moving inventory.

RJ Enterprises also had a service component to its business. Dean loved the service side. He again started with sales—to understand how orders came in, how they were priced, how service tickets or projects were executed and managed, and how profitability tracked on each one. The company really didn't have a good system for tracking this—another note made by Dean.

Dean also spoke with both the production and service teams about their equipment. He was interested in equipment utilization—how many days per year each piece of equipment was used, whether in production or service. He then worked with Rick to understand the revenue and margin each piece of equipment generated each year. There was a ratio there that Dean was looking for.

He also wanted to understand how people were utilized on the service side. RJ Enterprises didn't track personnel utilization or have a formal job costing process. Another note by Dean.

Next, Dean went into Sally's world—the back office. Sally was great. She and Dean worked really well together. They looked at everything—how customers were billed, how accounts receivable were handled, how payroll was processed, how accounts payable were managed, and ultimately, how all of that flowed into the general ledger, which fed the accounting reports.

Dean was extremely well-versed in all aspects of accounting. However, his goal was not to do the accounting but to mentor Sally. Dean was always there to answer her questions, and he would review the financial statements each month. When he found something that needed correcting, he usually taught Sally how to fix it—and that helped her grow immensely in her role. Dean knew that while she would never have the expertise to be a true CFO, she could be an outstanding office manager or controller.

* * *

As Dean and Rick began working together, their weekly one-on-one meetings were key. They talked about what was going right and what was going wrong.

Rick shared every concern he had with Dean, and Dean asked a lot of questions. Sometimes their one-on-one meetings lasted three or four hours. It wasn't unusual for their conversations to go well past when everyone else in the office had gone home.

When it came to Full Financial Control, Dean certainly took the lead. But what he did wasn't limited to the numbers side. Dean understood that while the CFO role had oversight of accounting (the past), most of what he focused on was finance (the future). When people asked what CFO stood for, Dean always said the title was Chief Financial Officer, but the role was all about Cash Flow, Finance, and Operations.

* * *

From Rick's standpoint, it took several months, but he was finally able to move away from being buried in admin work and toward the revenue side (sales and marketing), where his passion lay. As he started to gravitate toward his Unique Ability, Dean encouraged Rick to read Dan Sullivan and Dr. Benjamin Hardy's book *10x Is Easier Than 2x*, and he gave him a copy.

Early on, Rick gathered his key managers and explained what he was trying to do. He told them it would be a hard transition for him, but he was determined to make it work. Rick explained that they would begin to have weekly leadership meetings.

Dean was familiar with EOS, or the Entrepreneurial Operating System, made famous by Gino Wickman in his book *Traction: Get a Grip on Your Business*. As a result, Dean was always in their weekly leadership meetings, and they gradually moved into an EOS Level 10 Meeting (L10) format, with Dean facilitating.

Dean was by no means an expert in EOS but knew the basics. He also had a great relationship with a local EOS Implementor named Andrew, who volunteered to come in and help them get their L10 meetings started. That was also a great way for Rick to begin building a relationship with an EOS Implementor and to start learning more about EOS. Andrew also gave Rick copies of both *Traction* and *What the Heck Is EOS?*

* * *

The progress was slow, but that was intentional on Dean's part. He knew that for an organization of RJ Enterprises' size and maturity, it was best not to push the team too hard. Dean and Rick always had a list of issues they wanted to tackle, but they only addressed two or three during each ninety-day planning cycle. Dean knew trying to do more would overwhelm the company—and Rick.

Kate stopped by regularly to check in. Dean also worked hard to get Rick's other advisors more involved, and he introduced new ones when specific needs arose.

But what Rick really started to notice was his schedule—and how he felt about the business. He was finding the right balance between his family and his work. Rick's passion for the business was coming back.

* * *

Dean saw Annie several times each year—always at the company summer picnic in July, the holiday party in December, and occasionally when she stopped by the office on Tuesdays when Dean was there. She was always full of encouragement for Rick.

The first time Dean met Annie, when Rick introduced them, she shook his hand. Every time after that, when Annie saw Dean, she hugged him and softly said, "Thank you."

Early on, after each hug, Dean noticed Annie wiping a tear from her eye as she walked away. But over time, those tears turned into big smiles.

She was getting her husband back.

17

Three Years Later

TO SAY THAT Dean changed Rick's life would be an understatement.

Over the past three years, as Dean worked with Rick, Kate noticed changes every time she stopped by RJ Enterprises. While pictures from the early days were still around, over time, more and more pictures of Rick with his employees and customers were added to the walls.

New customers, better products, improved services, and many happy faces.

Kate sat down in the conference room where she and Rick had met for years. She continued to meet with Rick. And now, when they met, Dean was there too.

The business was growing, and Rick's management team was evolving, taking on leadership roles to help run the company.

Most of all, Rick was doing what he loved.

As they talked, Kate noticed Rick had an old notebook with him. It was well-worn, and she could tell it was several years old. Kate asked about it.

Rick opened the notebook to a page with a paper clip on it. He said the notes were from his first meeting with Dean, which had taken place just over three years ago.

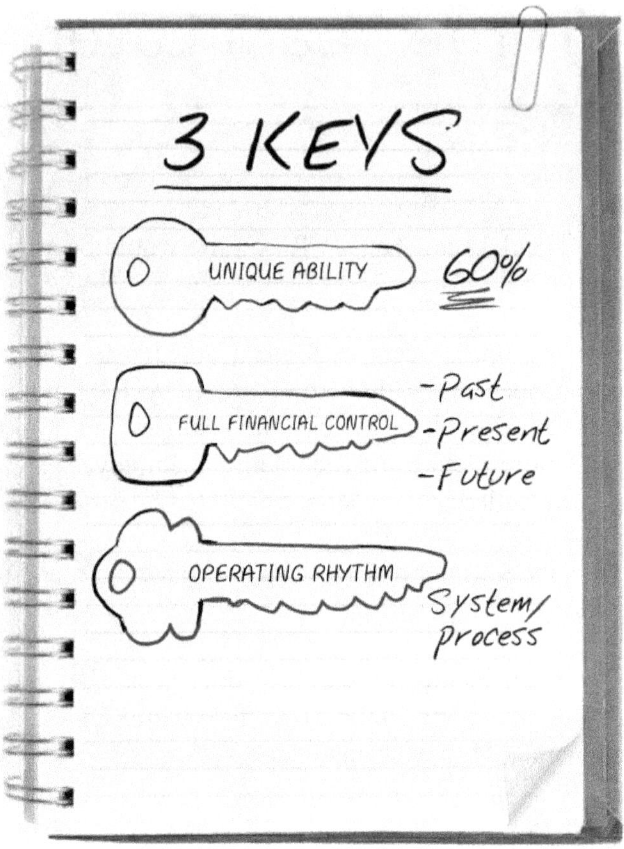

He told Kate he wanted to share with her one thing that Dean said early on. Something he didn't understand back then, but he understood it now. And it changed his life.

Kate glanced over at Rick's notebook. It was worn and tattered, and you could tell Rick had flipped back to these pages many times. As Rick began to speak, he didn't even need to read the words on the paper. He quoted each of them.

"The first is spending at least 60 percent of your time every week on your Unique Ability. The second is having Full Financial Control over every aspect of your business: past, present, and future. And third, is having an Operating Rhythm, a regular system or process of running your business, versus reacting to it all the time."

These were the three things that Dean had mentioned the first time he and Rick met. They had become the cornerstones of their work together.

Kate looked at Rick, then at Dean. "Guys, we've talked about part of this every time we have met, but can the two of you take me through what the journey has been like over these past three years?"

* * *

Rick spoke up. "First of all, do you remember how stressed I was about cash and getting the line of credit increased? That was my top priority when we met. And you said no to the increase."

"I didn't say no," said Kate, smiling. "I said not now."

"Well, to me it was a no," Rick countered. "But I can't thank you enough for saying no. One of the first things Dean worked on was my cash forecast. He did a thirteen-week cash flow projection.

"The projection showed us several things we could do to fix the cash crunch we were in. We pushed on collections, changed how we invoiced, looked at how we managed inventory, and then, in a real shocker to me, Dean helped me understand that some of our equipment was underutilized enough that we could sell it and generate cash.

"We did that, and between the proceeds from selling the equipment, the collections, and some changes in how we ordered inventory, the cash flow crunch went away. We were able to ramp up the new orders without any problem. We didn't even need the line of credit increase like I thought we did."

Rick paused for a moment, recalling the desperate place he was in during that meeting, before he continued. "I do know that if you had just given me the credit line increase, I would have simply borrowed against the line without fixing any of my existing problems."

Kate smiled. "That is what I was hoping would happen. More access to credit is not always a good thing."

Dean weighed in, "You would have just become a bigger company with bigger problems. The same problems you always had, just larger and harder to manage."

Rick looked down at his notes. "Well, I know that now. One of the things Dean always stressed is that growth isn't free. It takes cash and, more importantly, cash flow.

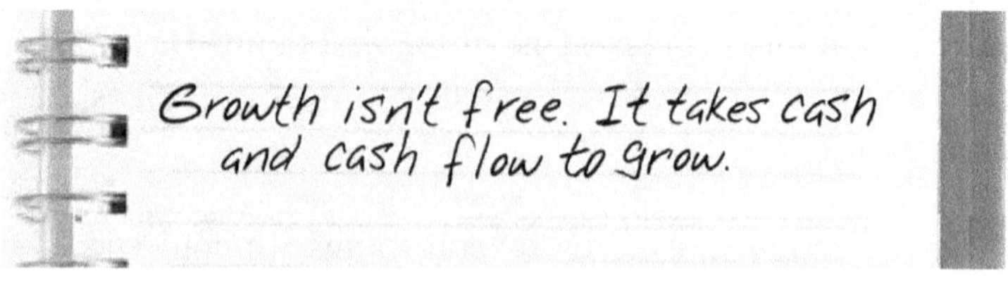

He then went on. "Dean always emphasized that there are three places for a business to get cash. The first is from investors. In the early days, that was me, and over time, I was tapped out—I put everything in that I could. The second is from the bank. And then third, from the business itself.

"We simply needed to make the business the primary source of our cash flow, which we did, versus running to the bank every time we needed more cash."

"Well said, and great job," Kate said with a bigger smile. "So, take me through what came next."

Rick went on.

"When Dean mentioned the three keys to success to me the first time, honestly, I didn't know what any of them meant. They were new concepts for me. But I knew what I wanted for the business, and I knew we had to do something different. So, I jumped in with both feet.

"As we got started, Dean told me that we couldn't tackle all three of them at the same time, but we needed to start with two of them. Starting with two would allow them to play off each other and build momentum. The third would fall into place gradually, and that was exactly what happened."

18

Gaining Full Financial Control

DEAN NODDED WHILE Rick explained the process, and then stepped in to add his insights. "We started with Full Financial Control and Unique Ability. Since Rick didn't have a leadership team, achieving a full-fledged Operating Rhythm would take time. The basics of an Operating Rhythm during the first eighteen months were the one-on-ones I had with Rick each week."

Rick's eyes flickered with excitement as he jumped in. "Let me say that even though it wasn't a full Operating Rhythm, those one-on-ones in the early days were critical to me. We had them every week when Dean was in. They were usually thirty to forty-five minutes long, and they helped me establish some personal accountability.

"It was a time for me to bounce ideas off of Dean. Sometimes we even went for hours. They were critical. And they became the highlight of my week."

"Mine as well." Dean smiled. "I knew, as the CFO, I could take the lead on Full Financial Control because that would free up Rick's time for his Unique Ability, which is certainly sales and business development. Even though he doesn't like parts of it, he likes most of it, and the reality is he is a natural and incredible at it."

Dean continued, "One of the first things I did was work with Sally to restructure the accounting reports, so they became more operationally focused and less accounting focused. We have expanded the reporting above gross profit to include revenue and direct costs, providing more detail. We then restructured overhead costs by department, including indirect costs, sales and marketing, production equipment, facilities, and general overhead.

"That exercise gave us the foundation we needed to look at the past, present, and future in a similar manner."

Dean went on, "The DNA Model, which is what we call the forecast model, then became the critical part of the business—the future. It is a rolling forecast, updated monthly in a spreadsheet, covering the next twenty-four months. When we close each month, we update the model from forecast to actual for that month, then add another forecast month to the end, so we are always forecasting twenty-four months ahead. And we forecast everything we can, at a very detailed level. That's why we call it a DNA Model."

Rick asked if he could comment. "It was interesting to watch. Dean would forecast all components of revenue, direct and indirect costs, and then department overhead costs at a detailed level, specifically by person. That was important because it was how I thought about the business. It all made sense to me."

"We also took a hard look at both maintenance and growth expenditures," Dean said, "because we knew we had some equipment that needed to be replaced, plus we needed to add additional capacity. We would then add the actual payments on existing term loans, the new term loans required for equipment purchases, income taxes, and any planned profit distributions. That level of detail always gave us visibility into what our cash flow and banking needs would be, in terms of working capital, equipment financing, and the line of credit."

Kate jumped in. "I can't tell you how much that helped in allowing me to get you the financing you needed to grow. It was so different than the old days, Rick, when you just told me you needed an increase in your line. My underwriters know that, given the detail you are able to provide us on both the history and the future, you have a complete grasp of the business, especially the numbers. That certainly makes it easy for us to get credit approved."

"Then came the present," Dean said with a smile. "With the past from the accounting system being presented in a way that made sense, and the future sketched out in the DNA Model, we started to work hard on the metrics. These are the Key Performance Indicators we will use to run the business. Over time, we incorporated more KPIs into the DNA Model to make it more intuitive for forecasting and updating.

"Rick and I then started to review the KPIs every week when we met. Those ultimately evolved into the weekly scorecard that the management team reviews and essentially runs the business around.

"We are now even talking about linking the KPIs to the incentive comp plan for Rick's key employees, as well as the overall financials."

"We have gotten to the point," Rick explained, "where we don't even need the accounting reports to know what the prior month will look like when we close the books. We know from the scorecard and the metrics."

After giving Dean an appreciative nod, he looked back at Kate. "I think back to when I used to tell you that I wasn't an accountant. None of this is accounting. It is just understanding the business and being able to use numbers to help you understand what is going right and what needs correcting."

Rick continued, "Dean has worked hard to help us develop the metrics around how I think about the business. Early on, one of the questions he asked me was, 'How do you know if you had a good day?' That was easy for me to answer, and many of our metrics are based on it. Today, I have a clear understanding of the distinction between accounting and finance. Accounting is the past. Finance is the future and looking ahead."

Dean added, "We use finance and our understanding of both sales and marketing, and production and operations to develop our plan for the future. I can't even tell you how many scenarios we run on the future. We have ideas; we discuss them, think they sound good, and then plug them into the forecast model. Sometimes when we look at the results, which are almost always tied to future cash flow, we don't like what we see, so we decide to go another direction."

Everyone laughed.

"You actually do have Full Financial Control at this point," said Kate. "So, tell me about Unique Ability."

19

Focusing on Unique Ability

RICK WAS QUICK to lean forward and speak up. "I can't even tell you how much fun this part is. It took some time, but as Dean began to take ownership of everything related to finance, accounting, and the admin side, I started to get my life back.

"Over time, I got to where I had at least two free days a week—every week—that I could do what I wanted. Days that I had been bogged down with the back-office stuff.

"Sure, I still interact with Sally since Dean isn't here every day, but that is for day-to-day things relating to what is going on in the business. I don't have to worry about the hard stuff. Dean takes care of all of that. And Kate, I can't tell you how much Sally loves working with Dean and how much she has personally grown. It is amazing."

"So how hard was it to let go?" asked Kate. "I mean, some of those things you have been doing since the beginning."

"Honestly, some were easy and some harder," replied Rick. "But it was the things I wasn't good at that were taking the most time and that were the most frustrating. Dean and I would talk about something, and he would have a few ideas on how to either simplify something we were doing or just bring a whole new idea to the table that we had never considered. As we started implementing those changes, tasks that used to take me two or three hours suddenly took someone else less time. At first, letting go was hard, but over time it became liberating.

"And then we just started to chip away at my schedule. At one point, Dean asked me to keep track of my time every day and log what I was doing. That was really eye-opening. It didn't take long for me to have a day back a week. Then two days a week. Then three. And I am working on more."

Kate smiled at Dean.

"So, with that time back, I was able to focus on customers. And when that happened, I felt like a new man." Rick sat up a little straighter in his chair. "I started to get up every day and do what I wanted to do. Even on Tuesdays when Dean was here for the day, I was usually out of the office at the beginning of the day. I would catch him at some point in the day for our one-on-one, but I certainly didn't need to be here all day with him. With me focused on the sales side, my operations time was really efficient because I was so familiar with what was going on in the business."

Kate noticed the enthusiasm in Rick's voice and asked a question she already knew the answer to. "What happened next?"

Almost before she could finish, Rick was quick to interject, "Everything that could go right started to go right. I think back to how much time I had been spending on running the business, or better said, letting the business run me. Once Dean took over all things related to finance, and I was free to focus on what I wanted to do, everything changed. And I loved what I was doing."

Dean said, "Kate, while there are always great results when a business owner focuses on their Unique Ability, I have found that if their Unique Ability can be directed towards sales or marketing or growth, it is amazing for me as a CFO to see what happens to the business. And it almost always happens fast!"

Rick smiled. "Sales is what I love to do." Then he added, "But Kate, here is the part that blew me away. Do you remember when you first suggested I have a fractional CFO? Do you remember my hesitation?"

Kate replied, "Sure. You said what everyone says. 'I can't afford it.'"

Rick replied, "Correct. But what I found was that as soon as I focused on the sales side—specifically, spending more time with customers and improving margins—both revenue and cash flow started to rise almost immediately. It was more than enough to pay for the cost of Dean."

Rick confidently nodded as he was speaking and continued, "Soon it was a 2x return. Then 4x. Then 8x. Then more.

"I realized we were already incurring the cost of Dean because we were so inefficient. Essentially, once Dean helped us address those inefficiencies, our investment in him was repaid. And then soon after that, it was an investment with a strong ROI."

Dean added. "And Rick was great. He went all in. Sometimes, business owners get hesitant and start to back away.

"But not Dean."

20

Developing an Operating Rhythm

KATE SAT BACK in her chair, smiling proudly at Rick.

Rick said, "Let me touch on Operating Rhythm. As things progressed over the first eighteen months, we began to dedicate time to focusing on the organization. In addition to my one-on-ones with Dean, we started with the Climb the Mountain Operating Rhythm process, which got us going. That was an important first step for us.

"In addition, Dean knew EOS pretty well. So in addition to our one-on-ones during that first year, we started to work on our organizational structure and use The Accountability Chart tool from EOS, which is different than a traditional organizational chart."

Rick then shared what he had learned. "I quickly realized that some of the people who worked with me in key roles—and don't get me wrong, they are great people—weren't the right ones to get me where I wanted to go. I thought that was the case even before Dean started, but it quickly became more apparent.

"Today, we are starting to formally put EOS in place as our Operating Rhythm. We've done some EOS self-implementing so far, but I know we are not doing it right. We are holding some basic Level 10 Meetings and starting to think about our EOS Vision/Traction Organizer (V/TO).

"But next week, we are meeting with Andrew, an EOS Implementor Dean introduced to me early on, to take a big step towards getting our Operating Rhythm rolling across the entire organization. He will officially begin working with us as our Implementor. I'm excited about that."

Kate smiled.

Rick continued, "One of the other things Dean always talks about was the importance of not only strategy and execution but also the middle step that almost every entrepreneur skips."

Kate asked curiously, "What's that?"

Rick looked at Dean, smiled, and said, "Structure."

Dean took the opportunity to go to the whiteboard in the conference room. He drew a graphic.

Dean then said, "Way too many people, entrepreneurs especially, get an idea, formulate a strategy, and then jump right into 'Let's go do this.' While that can work when a business is small, and the entrepreneur is handling all execution themselves, it falls apart when the entrepreneur tries to involve others in the execution.

"That's why structure is so important, and where EOS does such a great job in looking at structure with The Accountability Chart. It forces you to look at the organization in terms of roles, not people."

Rick jumped in, "Dean asked me to start looking at the organization that way when we first met – roles, not people. I had a great team—many of whom had been with me from the beginning—but they didn't have the capacity to do what I needed them to do as we grew and needed to move the business forward. In most cases, we found other roles for them in the company as we added others to our leadership team that could grow with us."

"That is a win-win," said Kate.

"For sure," Rick added. "Oh, and one last thing. I know you know this, but I have to say it. What Dean brought to the table was way more than numbers. It was how to run a business. He had learned so much from his business career working for those great, larger companies. It was invaluable to me. And it's funny to think back now, but none of those companies he worked for were in my industry.

"In the beginning, I wasn't sure about that. Now, looking back, it was the best thing that could have happened. He brought best practices and ideas from other industries to our business. Wow. It's been life-changing."

21

Creating Sustainable, Transferable Business Value

KATE SMILED. SHE was impressed. Impressed not only by what Dean and Rick had accomplished, but more so by how comfortable Rick was talking about the business side of the business. She asked, "So what's next?"

Rick was quick to jump in. "One of the things that has been so eye-opening to me is that I always thought that the numbers side of the business was just about accounting. You explained to me early on the difference between accounting and finance. Dean built on that by helping me understand that numbers are a key to business and that I needed to know my numbers. Numbers—the right ones—are a significant part of how value is created in business.

"One of the tremendous things Dean brought to the table is the Value Pyramid framework. The Value Pyramid is amazing. It completely changes the way you think about creating value in your business. And what Dean has taught me is that creating value is all about having *options*. It's not about selling.

"As you know, we started this journey with one of our three primary goals being to have Full Financial Control over the business—the past, present, and future. However, Dean helped me understand that the real goal goes much deeper—to build a business with sustainable, transferable business value.

"Dean showed me that as we worked through the Value Pyramid levels—Foundation Health Growth Value—we would create sustainable, transferable value in the business, and I would have *options*. In the beginning, I didn't understand that at all. But today I do. And while we are not fully there yet, I know that day is coming."

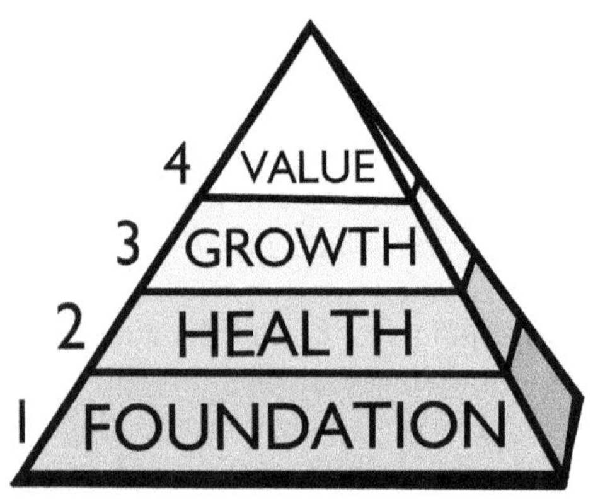

Rick continued, "The Value Pyramid starts with that solid Foundation of baseline accounting and cash flow tools that are critical to any business. I thought I had at least the accounting part working when I first met Dean. However, I learned that while Sally was doing her best, our accounting was, I must admit, slow and not always accurate. Dean helped her with that and documented the basic processes we use across the company. Sally is now Dean's biggest fan because of how much he has helped her and how much she has learned.

"Foundation then gets into having meaningful relationships with my attorney, banker, and CPA. I always had that with you, Kate, but not so much with my attorney and CPA. I just viewed them as people who did things I didn't like to do: contracts and taxes. Dean stressed the importance of involving these three key advisors in my business so they could help me, and they now do. I meet with my attorney and CPA at least twice a year so they can learn more about the details of my business, just like I regularly meet with you. This allows them to be proactive in bringing fresh ideas to the table that help our business. Things I never would have thought to ask for."

Rick went on, "Dean, can you share with Kate what we have done at the Health level?"

Dean jumped in. "I love to talk about Health because that is where we as CFOs live. Having a healthy business is all about having the tools and information to know how you did yesterday, how you are doing today, and what you will do tomorrow. Metrics and Key Performance Indicators are critical in every aspect of the business. These become part of the weekly scorecard. We look for trends and take action immediately when we identify problems.

"Rolling operating and cash flow forecasts then give us visibility into the future. We are always looking at sales, gross margin, EBITDA, and cash flow to make sure we know what is coming."

Dean paused for a few seconds before continuing. "But to tell the truth, I am not a huge fan of EBITDA by itself because it doesn't take into account working capital changes. I much prefer looking at Cash Flow from Operations, which is a line item on the cash flow statement that includes changes in working capital. We always ensure we look hard at Cash Flow from

Operations in the DNA Model. But because EBITDA is so commonly used these days, we always want to look at it, as well."

Rick nodded. He had heard the same thing from Jack in Chicago, but he didn't understand it back then. Today, he did.

Dean continued. "We also look hard at the business's capital structure, which includes both bank debt and the possibility of bringing in outside capital, if we were to ever need that.

"Plus, we will make sure Rick's team of outside advisors starts to include strong insurance contacts for both business insurance and all aspects of employee benefits."

Kate had heard this from Dean before, and she loved hearing it again. "It's so great to hear you talk about this. I find that so many businesses just skip this level altogether. Too often, they don't even have the Foundation working right, and they skip right over Health and try to just add sales."

Dean smiled. "And you know what they end up with. They start with an unhealthy business and end up with an even bigger unhealthy business."

Everyone nodded. Rick was quick to say, "And that was almost me."

Rick continued, "As Dean then helped me understand Growth, he helped me understand the key was not simply growth, but healthy and profitable growth. It starts with strong profit margins on everything we do.

"Before, I didn't know my margin on any of our products and services. I thought I did, but I was just guessing. And in reality,

I just sold what I knew people would buy. I was chasing sales and not profit.

"As Dean delved into our gross margins, we gained a deeper understanding of the true margin on everything we did. That forced us to either adjust pricing to achieve the right profit margin on every product and service we sold, or stop selling some things because we weren't making enough on them. That made some customers unhappy, but it was the right thing to do.

"Then, to take it to the next level, we started to look at not only our gross margin by customer but also our cash flow by customer. Wow, that was eye-opening to me. We found that as we steered towards high-margin products and customers with good payment terms, the cash started to come in. I hate to admit it, but we had some customers who were both low-margin and slow payers, and they were causing the bulk of our cash flow problems. Most of them are no longer customers."

Dean jumped in, "Growth also gets into strategic planning and making sure Rick has a good wealth and estate planning advisor. Growth can also involve examining potential acquisitions, where Rick either acquires another company in his industry or expands his product or service offering through an acquisition, if we decide to do so.

"And as we all know, we have to be cautious if we decide to go that route. And we would never make an acquisition without the Foundation and Health levels working well; otherwise, we would fail to integrate it. But if we do decide to do an acquisition or two, Kate, that's where we will need you."

"We stand ready to help with financing, if you need it," Kate replied. "Your numbers are so strong now, it would be great to look at something if you decide to acquire another business."

"And lastly, is the Value level," said Rick. "Dean has started to help me understand how potential buyers look at companies like mine, including the difference between financial buyers and strategic buyers. We have also talked about an ESOP as a possible option down the road for RJ Enterprises."

Kate nodded. She was impressed by what she was hearing from Rick and glanced at Dean. He looked like a proud papa.

Rick went on. "I still have a lot to learn about all of this and how business valuation actually works. I now laugh when I hear some of my friends at the golf club talk about how much they think their business is worth. I don't think they have a clue.

"And I appreciate that Dean's team has a dedicated group of CFOs with significant transaction experience who serve as a resource to both Dean and me. They have been through hundreds of transactions and stand ready to help."

Dean nodded. "I've talked to them already to learn a little more about some of these options. I'm not a transaction expert, but I know I have a team of them ready to help. They are just a phone call away."

"I love it, and it's all very impressive," said Kate. "It's something you don't see from solo fractional CFOs or even from smaller fractional CFO groups, where the CFO you work with is limited to only what they know from their personal experience."

She then asked, "So, what's next?"

22

Next Steps and Having the Right Advisors

RICK THOUGHT FOR a second before he continued, "I've had a few friends ask me if I want to sell the business. I just laugh. I have heard other people talk about doing that or having done that. But right now, I'm not looking to sell at all. I started the business because I wanted to make a real difference and do what I love. To be in control of my life and to give my employees a chance to have a great life.

"And today, I have a business that I love, and I love what I do. I have a great team, and we are constantly improving."

Kate nodded and said, "It's amazing to see."

Rick added, "But let me just say this because it's really important. What has stood out to me the most, and Dean has said this repeatedly, is that creating Value doesn't mean you have to sell your business. It means you have *options*. One option I really like is spending the next five to ten years running my business, having fun, being in control, and then seeing what the future holds.

"But having said that, we have started to take the right steps to make sure Annie and the kids will be okay if anything were to happen to me. This includes keyman and buy-sell life and disability insurance, current wills, and the basics of estate planning.

"Plus, and this is important too, we are now working on an operational transition plan for the business in the event something happens, and I am no longer around. The financial side isn't too hard to plan for with the right advisors. But the operational plan for the business—who will take over and how it will continue to run—is much harder. Dean would certainly be there to quarterback the transition, but we want to have a framework for what the business would do."

Rick looked at Dean and then at Kate. "These aren't things you want to think about, but they are really important. I have a responsibility not only to my family, but also to my employees."

Kate thought for a moment, then she said, "It really is fantastic to hear you talk about this. I know it's something you never want to envision, but I have seen some situations where the planning wasn't done, something terrible happened, and both the owner's family and the employees all suffered."

Dean added, "I agree 100 percent—and I'm grateful that Rick has trusted me enough to talk about all of this.

"That said, there's also a really positive side to what we've been discussing and the advisors I have been able to introduce to Rick.

"We all know that as a business grows and gains value, there are some really important things every owner should start to think about. Even though Rick doesn't have any plans to sell, we've met with a business advisor who specializes in helping business owners understand business valuation and what is involved in selling a business."

Rick thought back to Chicago and Jack's presentation.

Dean continued, "We want to make sure Rick knows the right wealth advisors, CPAs, attorneys, and other professionals—so that if the business ever outgrows any of Rick's current advisors, he's already connected to the right people. Rick has started to make some of those connections around town."

Rick chimed in, looking at Kate, "Dean certainly has me thinking about the long-term and planning for it. I am starting to think about the end goal and working backwards, versus thinking just about where I am now."

Rick paused for a long moment and then continued, "And all of this is a world I didn't even know existed. It's been incredible to meet these advisors and learn what they do.

"It's funny—but not really. Before you introduced me to Dean, Kate, I remember constantly worrying about the cost of advisors. I was always asking about hourly rates.

"I've since learned that the true 'cost' of advisors is what they don't know or haven't seen. It's always best to have experts—people who have been there, and done that—advising you. The cost of bad advice—or no advice—is never worth it."

Rick was clearly excited when he said, "And best of all, I am learning so much about *business*."

Kate was quick to say, "Rick, this is such a great place for you to be."

After another long pause, Dean leaned forward and said, "Kate, you know none of this would have happened if it weren't for you."

Kate looked away humbly.

Rick said, "Kate, I didn't even know what a CFO was, let alone that I could get one in a way I could afford. I thought my CPA was the same as a CFO. Or that Sally could be my CFO. I laugh now when I think about either of those misconceptions."

Kate jumped in. "Let me just say that you guys have done an amazing job, and I appreciate hearing the whole story. "

Lots of smiles. Lots of hugs.

* * *

As Kate stood up to leave, she thought back to that day three years earlier when she knew Rick needed help. She used to worry about how to get business owners to meet with someone like Dean. Today, when she sees they are frustrated, she knows all she has to do is ask.

She has found over the years that business owners will talk to someone when a trusted advisor asks them to.

23

A CEO Peer Group

AS DEAN AND Kate walked out of RJ Enterprises and into the late afternoon sun, they paused for a moment near their cars.

Kate glanced over. "He really seems like he's in a good place."

Dean nodded. "Much better. You can see it in how he carries himself. Still a long way to go, but he's gaining traction."

"He's lucky to have you," Kate said.

Dean shook his head. "He's lucky to have you. You were the one who told him the truth when it counted. Most bankers would have simply pushed through the credit line and walked away."

Kate smiled. "Well, I knew what he really needed. And now you're giving it to him."

Dean tucked his notebook under his arm. "You know what else? He's looking at joining a CEO peer group."

Kate looked at Dean. "A CEO peer group. What a great idea. How did that come up?"

Dean grinned. "We talked about it a few weeks ago. I mentioned how helpful it can be for business owners to have a peer

———

115

group—a circle where they can talk openly with other business owners, wrestle with challenges, and get a real-world perspective from people who get it. He got quiet for a while after that. Then he wrote it down in his notebook. I think it stuck."

Kate nodded slowly. "That actually makes a lot of sense. He's been carrying so much on his own for years. Having a place where he can learn from other business owners—that could be a huge relief."

Dean smiled. "Exactly. A CEO peer group isn't about giving him another to-do list. It's about giving him space. Space to step back, reflect, and hear from other leaders who've walked the same path. It's one of the best investments a CEO can make—not in their business, but in themselves."

Kate leaned against her car door. "You know, I've seen it too. He listens more. He delegates better. And over these past few years that you have been working with him, he realizes he doesn't have to do it all alone."

Dean looked out across the parking lot. "He's starting to understand what a real support system looks like. He has Annie. He has you. He has me. And now, maybe he'll have a circle of peers who can help him by sharing their experiences by talking about their businesses."

Kate nodded. "Sounds like he's really getting his footing."

They both stood quietly for a moment, looking up at the bright sun in the warm July sky.

Dean turned to go. "Thanks again, Kate. You really did start all of this."

Kate smiled. "Maybe. But it's Rick who is taking the right steps."

———

24

Basketball

WHEN RICK LEFT the office that day, it was 4:00 p.m.

His son, Ryan, had started for the high school basketball team as a junior that past season. They'd made it all the way to the district finals in the state tournament, and now Ryan was playing in an AAU summer league. His team had a tournament game starting in an hour.

Rick would be there—as he had been for nearly every game over the past few seasons.

Emily, his daughter, was finishing eighth grade. Her musical talent—and her love for music—had blossomed in ways that still surprised him. Rick never missed a recital. He was always there, sitting proudly in the audience, smiling before she ever stepped on stage.

His babies were growing up.

He also had lunch scheduled later that week with Tom Miller and found himself looking forward to it. They had stayed close since Rick left Miller & Co., meeting a few times each year. Tom had hated to see him go, but he'd never stopped being proud of what Rick had built. Over the years, Tom had become more than a boss—he was a mentor, a steady presence, almost a second father.

Rick put his truck in drive and headed home. He turned on the radio.

Springsteen.

This time, "Better Days" was playing.

He rolled up to a traffic light and stopped, letting the song play. It took him back—back to that drive more than three years earlier, when The Boss's "The Promised Land" had rattled him. Back when he'd questioned everything: his choices, his sacrifices, whether the dream was slipping away faster than he could chase it.

But today felt different.

The fear was gone.

The uncertainty had loosened its grip.

The insecurity that once followed him everywhere no longer sat in the passenger seat.

The song carried a feeling of confidence. The kind that comes after making hard decisions, pushing forward in hard times, even after learning that progress doesn't mean there won't be struggles.

Rick smiled.

He understood something now that had taken him years to learn: in business, as in life, the road is never smooth and never easy. Growth brings complexity. Dreams bring pressure. And too often, the people carrying the weight of it all—business owners—try to climb alone.

They don't have to.

Rick had learned that success isn't about pushing harder in isolation. It's about finding help. About trusting someone to walk beside you. He had found his Sherpa—someone who helped him see more clearly, plan more intentionally, and climb higher than he ever could on his own.

The light turned green.

Rick eased forward and turned left.

He was headed to a basketball game.

Afterword

While this story centers on Rick (the business owner), Kate (his banker), and Dean (his fractional CFO), it reflects the experiences of so many business owners.

Rick's situation is fictional—but it's also real. Because it's happening everywhere. In fact, while each of the characters in the story is technically fictional, they are all very real. Each is a composite of people I have seen in action in my professional and personal life. Entrepreneurs. Trusted Advisors. CFOs. And behind the scenes, and often unseen, are families.

The story about Jack (not his real name), however, is true. I was at that conference and in that session in Chicago, sitting in the back, like I always did.

Rick was fortunate to have an advisor who genuinely cared. Kate happened to be a banker, but she could just as easily have been a wealth advisor, attorney, business coach, insurance broker, or CPA.

Every business owner has a handful of advisors. Some offer expertise. But some offer something more. Much more. Kate was one of those. She didn't just process a loan or extend a line of credit; she saw that Rick needed real help and made the right connection.

The reality is this. The CEO of a company with $200 million in sales almost always has an experienced leadership team. But the owner of a company with $2 million to $30 million in sales often stands alone—surrounded by loyal people but lacking deep experience.

That's where the fractional model changes everything. The smaller business CEO can now build a team of experienced C-suite leaders, just like their larger company counterparts, at a cost they can afford.

To entrepreneurs everywhere, always remember: while we are each the sum of our own personal experiences—and while we can all learn—what we know is never enough.

No one can do it alone.

And while every business must master all three areas: revenue, production, and finance/administration, no single person can be world-class in all three. Especially finance—often the most critical lever in both times of growth and times of stress—and almost always the hardest for so many business owners to grasp. That's why fractional CFOs are often the first and most valuable outside resource a business owner needs to add to their leadership team.

So, to business owners everywhere, if you already have a fractional CFO who is helping you like this, you trust them, and they are doing the right things for you, please stick with them. They are hard to find.

If we at FocusCFO can be of assistance, we'd be delighted to get to know you.

And if we don't meet you directly, hopefully one of your advisors will be like Kate and introduce us.

Clarifying the FocusCFO Model

In this story, Kate introduced Rick directly to Dean, a fractional CFO. That's how it works in some fractional models—but not at FocusCFO.

At FocusCFO, we use a unique model centered on an Area President—experienced industry veterans located in each market across the US where we operate—whose sole focus is market education and business development.

These include former entrepreneurs—many of whom have successfully started, grown, and exited their own businesses—as well as former bankers, finance leaders, and other seasoned professionals. They are highly entrepreneurial, understand the business issues that owners face, and what it takes to run a business.

Kate would have introduced Rick to a FocusCFO Area President—in this case, someone she knew locally. The Area President would have met with Rick, listened, asked questions, and then carefully selected the right CFO from the FocusCFO team for Rick based on skill set, personality, experience, and yes, sometimes industry background, though that's often overrated.

Many business owners and trusted advisors struggle to find a fractional CFO to work with. That is because solo fractional CFOs—those that operate on their own—and even many individuals within some larger fractional CFO groups, often work independently and usually only with a handful of businesses (three to five) at a time.

The challenge then is that many fractional CFOs are often "full" or at capacity, just when you need one. Or, sometimes the one you know might not have the right skill set for a particular business need. That means finding a fractional CFO—one who fits your needs AND has available time—is challenging.

The FocusCFO business model solves that issue. The extra person was just too hard to weave into the flow of the book, so I left it out. But in real life, this happens every time, and it's an easy part of our process.

Final Thoughts

As an entrepreneur myself, I know how hard the journey can be. You are not alone. It's hard for everyone. And it does take all three: Unique Ability, Full Financial Control, and Operating Rhythm.

As it relates to **Unique Ability**, first of all, a massive thank you to Dan Sullivan and the team at Strategic Coach for your groundbreaking work on entrepreneurial thinking and the concept of Unique Ability.

Personally, I discovered early on that my strengths were first in business development and later in building scalable training and go-to-market systems. Both fell within my Unique Ability, and I was fortunate to find them.

For most entrepreneurs, **Full Financial Control,** done right, is usually the hardest and ultimately limits their ability to grow.

I continue to meet regularly with business owners who struggle to achieve Full Financial Control. They have someone who does their numbers for them. But it isn't enough. That's why having a real, experienced, forward-looking, strategic CFO is so important. And again, I'm not talking about just giving your bookkeeper or controller the title. I am referring to someone who has the necessary experience to help you achieve your goals. That's why the fractional CFO model is so important for small and medium-sized businesses.

The Past is your accounting function. Your accounting reports. For those of you who remember newspapers, you might say they are yesterday's news. But the reality is they aren't even yesterday's news. Often, they are last month's news, or the news from three months ago, or, ugh, the news from last year.

And too often, if you are a small or medium-sized business and Sally is your controller or office manager, or you use an outside bookkeeper or CPA to do your accounting reports, they are not always accurate. In short, they are wrong. They need to be right. Not perfect. But right.

I have always said that while newer, easy-to-use accounting systems might be the best thing to ever happen to small busi-nesses, they are also the worst. Why? Today, everyone thinks they can prepare their own financial statements by hitting the print button. And that they are accurate. That is rarely the case. And believe me, your financial statements need to be accurate.

The Present is about right now. It is a set of metrics, or KPIs (Key Performance Indicators), that show how your business did yesterday, how it is doing today, and how it should per-form tomorrow. Sometimes these are called Flash Reports or Scorecards.

There are two types of metrics: leading indicators and lagging indicators. Leading indicators tell you about important things before they happen. Lagging indicators tell you after they have happened.

For example, the number of sales calls made last week is a leading indicator. It is an indicator of possible future sales. The number of orders booked last week is a lagging indicator. It tells you about the sales that happened last week.

Both are important, but you need the right mix. Usually, you want more leading than lagging. Regardless, they tell you things before you get your accounting reports, which is why both are important. And if you have the right ones, you can get ahead of waiting for your accounting reports.

A strong argument can be made that with the right metrics, you really don't need to rely on your accounting reports to know how your business is performing. It's actually true. You should know what your financial statements will look like before your accounting even gets done.

Something I have asked business owners to help them understand this concept is simply, "How do you know if you are having a good day (or week or month)?"

Most can rattle off six to eight things that they try to keep their finger on the pulse of on a day-to-day basis. Those can become your first set of metrics.

The Future is what we at FocusCFO call a DNA Model. It is almost always done in a spreadsheet and provides a very detailed, robust forecast of what you expect to happen in your business over the next 12 to 24 to 36 months. We call it a DNA Model because it is based on the building blocks of the businesses. The revenue drivers, the cost structure, and the cash flow cycle. When you isolate each one, you can run different scenarios and see the results. A good forecasting model is always based on cash flow, not net income. We like to describe it as being similar to the map on our phones or the GPS in our car. It is a roadmap of where we are going.

One of the reasons accountants (who often think of the past) struggle with finance (which requires you to think of the future) is that finance requires you to paint a picture of the future without all of the facts.

A CFO knows that a forecast is never "perfect," but the goal is to get it "directionally correct." If it has enough of the variables (i.e., the DNA) that you use to run your business (think metrics), you can use it to gain a fairly accurate prediction of the future.

But what it really does is emphasize the behaviors needed to drive the future toward the outcome you want. That leads to some of the things that are part of your Operating Rhythm: goals, scorecard items, and individual accountability. Ideally, most of these key drivers of future behavior are on your weekly scorecard or metrics report.

Just like your personal financial planner will do a long-term financial projection of your personal assets, your CFO does a long-term financial projection for your business.

Here is something I have never understood. It is true that most business owners still have a significant portion of their personal net worth tied up in their business. That means they don't always have all that much in investable assets outside their business (think cash). They often use a financial planner for their personal asset growth plan, which involves a smaller portion of their net worth. But they don't have a CFO to do the same type of financial planning for their business's growth plan, which involves much larger amounts of their personal net worth.

So past, present, and future. I hope you can see how it all starts to come together.

Jack, the investment banker at the Chicago conference, said it better than anyone when he simply asked all the business owners in the room, "How many of you have a CFO?" He wasn't talking about the office manager who does your bookkeeping, or a controller who does your accounting, or your outside CPA who does a financial statement. He was talking about a real, strategic CFO who knows your business inside and out, who understands your personal and business goals, and who matches your company's strategy with numbers. The one that creates a financial roadmap and a financial plan to help you scale your business.

Operating Rhythm took us much longer to master. I didn't even understand the concept of an Operating Rhythm until many years after I started FocusCFO. Personally, I love EOS, the Entrepreneurial Operating System, developed by Gino Wickman and outlined in his book *Traction: Get a Grip on Your Business*. EOS is simple, easy to understand, and by using it, a business can move as fast or as slow as it wants. You can "self-implement," meaning you read *Traction* and use the free tools outlined in the book. Or you can use an EOS Implementor, who can guide you through the process, run your quarterly and annual meetings, and who is a trained expert in using EOS.

At FocusCFO, we started using EOS in 2018, and it completely transformed our business. So much so that my personal story with EOS is included in Gino's book, *The EOS Life*, starting on page 83.

From the beginning of our EOS journey, we used an EOS Implementor. From watching other companies self-implement EOS, my observation is that while it works for a few, most are inconsistent, move too slowly, and generally start with the wrong things. But there is nothing wrong with giving it a try and implementing EOS yourself. Something is certainly better than nothing.

At FocusCFO, for clients who don't use an operating system, we often have them start with our Climb the Mountain Operating Rhythm system.

And there are other great operating systems out there. In the end, it matters less which system you use. What matters is that you use one and use it consistently. And that it makes a real impact on your business.

Bonus Section 1

---

12 Questions Every Business Owner Should Ask to Know If It's Time for a Fractional CFO

1. Are you getting timely, accurate, and actionable financial reports, or are decisions still being made in the dark?

2. Do you clearly understand your cash flow and have confidence that it will support your operations and growth?

3. Is revenue growing but profits flat or shrinking, without a clear explanation why?

4. Do you know which customers, products, or services are truly driving profitability, and which are draining it?

5. Do you have a trusted financial partner on your team, someone you can talk with openly about both numbers *and* strategy?

6. Does your leadership team understand the story behind the numbers, or is financial information still "locked up" in spreadsheets and jargon?

7. Are you getting the strategic forecasting, cash flow visibility, and forward-looking insights you need to make smart decisions?

8. Are you confident your company has the financial leadership, systems, and processes needed to scale?

9. Do you have a clear plan for building business value, one that aligns with your retirement, exit, or estate goals?

10. Is there a succession or transition plan in place that ensures continuity and protects the value you've built?

11. Are you spending too much time on day-to-day financial firefighting instead of focusing on growth and strategy?

12. Is your business helping you live the life you envisioned when you started it, or has it become a source of stress rather than freedom?

Bonus Section 2

12 Traits of Great Fractional CFOs

1. They think like an owner. Every decision is made with growth, value, and the long game in mind, not just short-term results.

2. They act as a true partner. Strategy isn't something they just talk about; they help connect the strategy and vision to the numbers and make sure the business is headed in the right direction.

3. Trust is at the center of the relationship. They're honest, transparent, reliable, and someone the owner can talk to about anything.

4. Teaching is part of the job. They raise the team's financial understanding, so decisions get better and confidence grows.

5. They make the complex simple. Numbers turn into clear stories and practical next steps that everyone can understand.

6. They bring discipline and focus. Budgets, forecasts, and priorities become tools that keep the company on track.

7. Collaboration comes naturally. They listen, work well with the team, and build alignment with advisors, banks, and partners.

8. They keep an eye on the road ahead and develop financial plans that look to the future. Forecasts and cash flow plans give the business visibility and help prevent surprises.

9. Hard conversations don't scare them. They speak the truth with empathy and guide the team toward the best decision.

10. Growth is always part of the conversation. They look for ways to improve profitability and build long-term value.

11. They adapt as things change. Fresh thinking and flexibility are part of how they operate. They bring new ideas to the table on a regular basis.

12. Their ultimate goal is sustainability. Everything they do is focused on helping the owner build a business that grows in value, is transferable, and supports whatever future the owner envisions.

Acknowledgments

I'm deeply grateful to Gino Wickman for creating the EOS framework, and to the many EOS Implementers who help business owners gain clarity and focus. While this book is not affiliated with EOS Worldwide, their principles have significantly influenced how I think about leadership, structure, and growth.

Thanks also to Dan Sullivan and the team at Strategic Coach for their groundbreaking work on entrepreneurial thinking and the concept of Unique Ability, which has helped thousands of owners—including me—focus on what we do best and build businesses we love.

Just as no business is built alone, this book was refined using a range of tools and support—including my editorial and design teams, my test readers, and limited AI tools that I personally used for drafting, content validation, and editorial review. The insights, decisions, and conclusions remain my own.

A special thank you to the team at Igniting Souls for your help and patience with me in getting this book published. To Heidi Peterson for your work on the cover design, which was probably harder for me than writing the book. And to Steve Campbell for your creative expertise with the illustrations.

And a huge shout-out to my daughter, Emily, who did her best to chase down and correct all of my typos and grammatical errors. It was a massive undertaking. As soon as she found the ones I had in the text and cleaned those up, I added a few more to keep her on her toes. And thank you to my wife, Michelle, and my youngest daughter, Annie, for helping with proofreading as well. I'm sure I managed to sneak in a few mistakes that the three of them still couldn't find.

Test readers, thank you for your contribution and insights in making this book better. I won't list each of your names, but know that I am proud to call all of you my friends.

To all of our FocusCFO clients, it has been incredible for each of us to learn from you and see the passion you have for your business. You are the Rick in this story.

And to so many of you who are our referral partners and have introduced us to your clients and business associates, we are so very appreciative of your trust in us and for making introductions. You are the Kate in the story.

And from the bottom of my heart, thank you to the team at FocusCFO for the work you do every day in support of business owners everywhere. Your commitment to helping owners gain financial control—and being true Sherpas—has inspired much of this story. You are the Dean in the story.

About the Author

Brad Martyn is an entrepreneur, husband, and a proud dad and grandpa. He and his wife, Michelle, live just outside of their hometown of Columbus, Ohio. They have five adult children and now enjoy a growing crew of grandchildren.

After nearly two decades working mostly in corporate finance and operations, Brad took a leap of faith at age forty, walking away from his corporate career to start FocusCFO. What began as a vision to give a handful of business owners greater financial control in their businesses has since grown into one of the largest fractional CFO organizations in the United States.

Along the way, Brad has met with hundreds of entrepreneurs and business owners, learning from their journeys and sharing insights from his own experiences. Today, with an experienced internal team now carrying FocusCFO forward, Brad spends much of his time in and around Central Ohio, sitting across the table from fellow entrepreneurs listening, advising, and encouraging.

He's seen firsthand the challenges—and rewards—of building something that lasts. And through it all, Brad has come to believe one thing deeply: no business owner should ever have to climb alone.

BradMartyn.com

More from Brad Martyn

I hope you enjoyed reading *Never Climb Alone*, the story about Rick, Dean, and Kate, and how Rick learned that building a business is never something you can do alone. And how Kate helped Rick understand that adding a fractional CFO to his team allowed him to focus on what was critical to the business, and what he truly loved to do.

The next book is *Tools for the Climb*. This is an in-depth look at the work Dean did as a fractional CFO during the first three years working with Rick. *Tools for the Climb* isn't a sequel to *Never Climb Alone*, but a deeper dive into what Rick and Dean worked on during those three years, from when Dean started to that meeting with Kate which marked a clear turning point. It explores the disciplines, decisions, and tools that helped transform effort into structure and growth into something sustainable.

Lastly, *Reaching the Summit* is the sequel to *Never Climb Alone* and will take the reader through what happens next. Dean and Rick continue to work together, and Rick makes the important decision to take his business, RJ Enterprises, to the next level. Here, Rick learns what it means to really build a business that has sustainable, transferable value, and how that decision pushes him completely out of his comfort zone. See the challenges and benefits as Rick moves into a role of true leadership, and how that change requires him to really let go and trust his team. The end result, however, is where so many entrepreneurs, including Rick, dream about getting to.

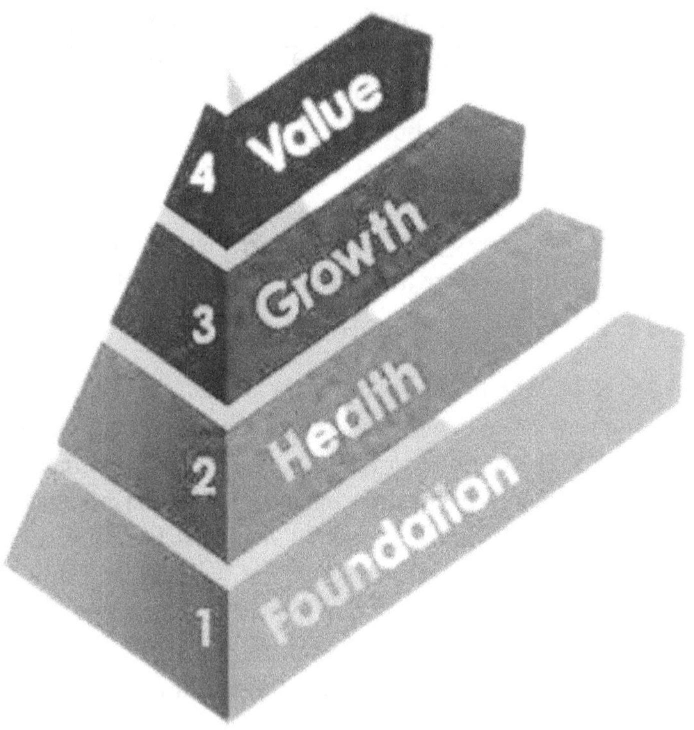

FocusCFO.com

If you are a business owner and would like to learn more about how a fractional CFO can help your business, or

If you are an experienced CFO or finance executive and are interested in learning more about becoming a fractional CFO.

Scan the QR code or visit
BradMartyn.com/contact
to learn more.

Suggested Reading List